Freestyle
Skiing

to Katy

Freestyle Skiing

a complete guide to the fundamentals of hot dogging

Randy Wieman

photography
Robbi Newman

Angus & Robertson Publishers

Colour photographs, unless otherwise acknowledged, are by the author.

ANGUS & ROBERTSON PUBLISHERS
London • Sydney • Melbourne • Singapore • Manila

First published by
Angus & Robertson Publishers, Australia, 1980
First published by
Angus & Robertson (UK) Ltd, 1979

© text Randy Wieman 1979
© black and white photographs Robbi Newman 1979

National Library of Australia
Cataloguing-in-publication data.

Wieman, Randy.
    Freestyle: a complete guide to the fundamentals of
    hot dogging.

    ISBN 0 207 14321 8 paperbound
    ISBN 0 207 13856 7 hardbound

    1. Skis and skiing. I. Newman, Robbi, photographer.
    II. Title.

796.93

Printed in Singapore by Toppan Printing Co. (S) Pte. Ltd.

contents

During the winter of 1973 I spent my first full ski season in the resort town of Davos, Switzerland, teaching skiing but still keeping plenty of time to ski myself. After this prolonged exposure to the wonderful joys of crisp mornings, powder snow and being the first up the mountain day after day, I felt that there had to be some way to be able to ski more and work less. The following season I entered my first freestyle competition in Leysin, Switzerland, and won the aerial event and 50 Suisse Francs, with a double Daffy. Within a week I had bought a pair of short skis and was practising ballet, attempting Helicopters and Flips. One year later I signed my first contract with a ski manufacturer. The days of being a professional freestyler had begun. From that point there has been no turning back. As freestyle skiing has grown, so have I.

My hope is that many other skiers will have a chance to be involved in the freestyle way of skiing. It doesn't take a total commitment, just a bit of effort. Every part of freestyle has its easy side, as well as its spectacular, and difficult side. Freestyle is much more than flips and hair raising descents through the moguls. There are basic manoeuvres in ballet that any intermediate skier can learn to perform. A skier can ski the bumps slowly and still use the principles that have been developed by the freestyle bump skiers. Even jumping is not as awesome as it seems. There are transitions and moguls on any hill that can provide the necessary lift for the small jump once the proper technique is acquired.

Freestyle skiing has come a long way since the Hot Dog days. It is now a highly developed extension of the sport of skiing. Freestyle schools have grown throughout the skiing world, teaching many of the fundamentals quickly and safely. No longer do freestylers let themselves simply try anything. Instead a progression is followed to arrive safely at a chosen goal.

This book has been written to explain the evolution of freestyle skiing and to give a basic understanding of what the sport is about. With the aid of the many sequential photos and descriptions of various tricks, it is hoped that readers will understand the freestyle learning process and not be afraid to give some of the tricks a try. Anybody who has skied a bit can get involved. I have met many skiers who have asked me questions about freestyle skiing and the learning processes involved. I hope this book will answer those questions as well as give others something new and exciting to try next time they are on skis. So loosen up, be free and ski free.

Randy Wieman

THE FREESTYLE STORY

The roots of present day freestyle skiing are deeply embedded in skiing's past. Its deepest roots reach down to the first traces of skiing 15,000 years ago in Siberia; a pair of skis found in Sweden which were used around 2500 B.C., and rock drawings found in Norway, depicting hunters on skis, which date back to 2000 B.C.

During the 1840s Sondre Norheim of Telemark invented the first modern ski by making it narrower at the middle than at both ends and the first modern bindings by adding extra straps so that the foot wouldn't sway from side to side. His new equipment enabled him to develop two new methods of turning. The first was called the Telemark and the second, the Christiania, named after the capital of Norway. Christiania later became Oslo but the term still means "turn" to the skier. Norheim's inventions made skiing easier for beginners as well as enabling the experts to develop improved techniques.

From Norway the sport spread out to many other countries. Norwegian miners began skiing in the mountains of America. No Norwegian miner is better known than John Thorensen, alias Snowshoe Thomsen. From 1856 until his death in 1876 Snowshoe carried mail 140 km over the Sierra Nevadas from Placerville in California to Genoa in Nevada, and back, to provide the only winter mail service between the east and California, with the exception of a ship service which took four months, travelling around the Cape of Good Hope. In 1870 Norwegian gold miners climbed Australia's highest mountain, Koscuisko, and skied down its slopes. They also took skis to New Zealand; but the sport didn't catch on at that stage. Much earlier the Vikings had transported skis to England while skis had also arrived in the Alps. The mountains' steepness made skiing impractical for all but a few intrepid souls.

In the late 1890s an Austrian officer by the name of Mathias Zdarsky developed a system of turning that was simple to learn and efficient enough to handle the steep slopes while patrolling Austria's mountainous border. It was called the Stem Christiania. The technique was greatly assisted by the use of shorter skis. Though some stability was lost when straight running, the shorter length made it possible to get the skis around on a steep slope. Later, in a town called Lillenfield, near Vienna, Zdarsky started what was probably the first formal ski school. His technique, combined with that of Telemark, produced a learning process which made skiing possible for many more people.

But it was the development of uphill transportation that brought the masses to the sport. By the beginning of World War II, Europe and America had several lift systems. For the most part they were small and short keeping skiers on the flatter slopes at the base of the mountains. When the war was over developments took off in many directions. New ski areas were opened up, with advanced lift systems. Howard Head, an aircraft engineer, developed his metal ski. Bob Lange produced the first buckle boot in 1965. Then, as more people achieved greater leisure time and had more money to spend, ski areas grew and advancements were made in skiing technique. In 1957 Clif Taylor helped develop a new method of ski instruction called GLM (Graduated Length Method). Using this system, skiers begin on very short skis, graduating progressively to the conventional length.

It was during the 1960s that the sport of freestyle skiing really began to take shape, although several significant events occurred earlier.

In 1929 Dr Fritz Reuel wrote a book entitled *New Possibilities in Skiing*, which proposed the use of figure skating techniques by skiers. In 1940 Jimmy Madden, twice an Olympic figure skater, invented what was later termed "Goon Skis". They were short skis, about one and a half metres long, with both ends equally turned up. He had the right idea but it didn't catch on. In 1953 Stein Eriksen popularised inverted aerials with spectacular weekly demonstrations of back and front flips. However, Stein wasn't the first to flip on skis. The first recorded aerial somersault was performed in Norway in 1907. America had its share of "flippers" too, but none perfected the skill anywhere near comparable to the standard achieved by Stein.

At least not until 1965 when an Austrian gymnast named Hermann Goellner began getting into the air. Goellner was the first skier to perform a double flip, and still one of the few to manage a triple. After that he had still one more trick up his sleeve, the moebius flip (a flip with a full twist).

Tom LeRoi, a skier with the reflexes of a cat, teamed up with Hermann to demonstrate simultaneous front and back flips, setting a standard for future aerial acrobats. Their talents were displayed in the film *Moebius Flip*, the first film on the subject of freestyle.

At about the same time ballet skiing was also in its early stages. During the early 1960s Doug Pfeiffer, future editor of *Skiing* magazine, developed the School of Exotic Skiing. Soon afterwards a Suisse named Art Furrer became involved in ballet and invented many of today's basic stunts such as the Tip Roll, Charleston, and Javelin Turn. Furrer was also featured in the film *Moebius Flip*. In Europe Heinz Garhammer of Munich had begun trick skiing, and Henri Authier of Tignes, France, was attempting any trick he could think of, not knowing that other skiers were doing the same sort of thing.

By 1970 there was quite a large underground following of what became known as Hot Dog skiing. This was the title given to the new "crazy" way of skiing and those that did it. Some people believe that the term "Hot Dogging" originated as a surfing term describing someone who took the most chances on a wave—a guy who was super aggressive. Others believe that Hot Dogging actually got its name on a ski slope. Legend has it that a skier was eating a hot dog at the top of an extremely steep run. As his hand squeezed around the bun so that he could get his first bite the hot dog shot out and, falling on the snow, started to wend its way through the moguls. Its line through the bumps was so good that the skiers started to follow its example and Hot Dog skiing was born.

Throughout America, Canada and Europe, small groups of skiers were breaking away from the traditional "racing" approach to skiing. They were letting go and attempting new things. The basics of Ballet, Aerials and Hot Dogging were there. When Tom Corcoran and Doug Pfeiffer organised the first freestyle competition at Waterville Valley, Vermont, the response was overwhelming. Hot Doggers from all over North America and Europe arrived to take part. Hermann Goellner, with his incredible flipping, won first prize—a Chevrolet Stingray. The next competition, at Vail, Colorado, was won by Fuzzy Garhammer who drove away

his first prize Chevrolet Camaro. These freestyle competitions were more successful than anyone had hoped for. It was the beginning of a sport that was destined to keep growing.

The winter of 1973 brought a change to the freestyle circuit in America where, up until then freestyle had been completely free. A competitor could do, just about, whatever he wanted so long as the judges and crowds liked it. Skiers were carefree and ready to try anything; especially when so much prize money was at stake. Spectacular crashes and recoveries were greeted by the spectators with wild cheers of "go for it" and "more air". No limit was known. Then two competitors were permanently paralysed while attempting difficult aerial manoeuvres. Many areas in America banned freestyle altogether and the competitors formed IFSA (International Freestyle Skiers Association) in order to preserve their sport. By banding together and placing high safety controls on each event, especially the aerials, the skiers ensured that 1974 had an injury free season with more prize money than ever. Bob Salerno proved to be the top dog and won $18,000.

Europe also had several freestyle competitions, the main one taking place on Jakobshorn in Davos, Switzerland. Ruedi Niggli won first prize—an Austin. Coronet Peak in New Zealand sponsored its first competition and the atmosphere was much the same as in the States three years before.

1975 saw the top European competitors coming back to their home ground. EFSA (European Freestyle Skiers Association) formed a circuit sponsored by Camel cigarettes which covered every country in the Alps. The tour ended at Cervinia with the first World Championships. Six thousand Italians came to watch the best freestyle competitors from America, Canada and Europe. Scott Brooksbank (USA) won the overall but Europeans were placed second in every event; Franco Zanolari in the bumps, Peter Lindeke in ballet, and Henri Authier in the air (with a back moebius for his first jump and a front moebius for his second).

The Americans and Canadians had to get back home to finish off their $200,000 circuit at Snowbird, Utah. Mark Stiegemeier ended up the men's overall winner for the season. After a successful winter of freestyle, competitors headed home to

train for what was to be the best season ever.
Freestyle competitions were everywhere in 1976. North America had two circuits—the Chevy Circuit and the PFA (Professional Freestylers Association) world tour. There were three in Europe sponsored by Colgate for the women and Midas for the men. Europe had a five competition circuit ending in Are, Sweden, a place not too far from the land of the midnight sun. Coronet Peak continued with its annual event and Scotland and Australia staged their first freestyle competitions.

The PFA had over $600,000 in prize money, to be divided equally between men and women. The $130,000 PFA world tour final in Snowbird, Utah, was the grand final to an incredible season. Marion Post won the women's overall for the season; with prize money of $29,000. Henri Authier won the ballet event with a mind boggling combination of acrobatics and grace. "Jumping Jack" won the aerials with three double back flips, beating Manfred Kastner (who had landed the circuit's first triple flip), because Kastner had fallen on one of his double flips. Ed Lincoln performed for the first time in competition a half in, half out (a double flip with a half twist in each flip). Triple helicopters and double flips were common. The 14,000 people who came to watch on that sunny day were not disappointed.

After Snowbird, competitors rushed to their summer camps to learn all the new tricks for the 1977 season. The Chevy circuit had collapsed so that would add more competitors to PFA. The top Europeans were also counting on PFA to come through with a good world tour, but that's not the way it worked out. Already late in the season, the first competition was held at Stratton Mountain, Vermont, in the middle of January. Over 200 competitors came to contest the 16 final spots in the women's event and men's event. Each entrant was asked to pay $500 for insurance and PFA fees. The Europeans having their own insurance and dues to pay, refused these additional fees and left to start their own circuit back home. This left the PFA without a world tour but they staged a U.S. tour. With insurance, promotion and legal problems, the PFA finished up with only 3 competitions for the men (two Canadians, John Eaves and Grey Athens taking first and second places respectively) and two competitions for the

women, with Marion Post proving herself once again to be the best. In Europe four competitions were held: two in France, one in Yugoslavia and the final in Are, Sweden. Coronet Peak, New Zealand, still had its annual competition and Australia put together a $15,000, four competition circuit sponsored by Amco Jeans.

Despite the problems with the professionals the lower levels of the freestyle hierarchy are doing better than ever. Summer camps are attracting record crowds and freestyle classes are busy introducing the sport to many new skiers. Amateur competitions have grown to the extent that there are often more than one hundred contestants. Acrobatic demonstrations on plastic as well as snow are touring the USA, Canada and Europe. Skiing has come a long way since Sondre Norheim amazed the crowds at Christiania with his new turn. Freestyle is a part of this evolution and there remains a big future ahead. Observing today's freestyle skiing, it is hard to believe that it can possibly go any farther, but it will—just wait till next year.

EQUIPMENT

Not even the invention of plastic boots or metal skis revolutionised the ski market as much as the development of freestyle skiing. Whilst such innovations and inventions completely changed one part of the ski industry, freestyle touched every facet of the skiing world, leaving nothing quite the same as before. For the first time in modern ski history the sport had a new direction: gone was the idea that everybody had to ski, dress and act like a racer to be "in" on the slope. There was another alternative and many skiers wanted to try it. Freestyle reminded everyone that skiing was fun and loose, not strict and formal. With freestyle competitors leading the way this feeling was generated to manufacturers and transformed into products that let skiers follow the freestyle spirit.

Competitors needed equipment that the market did not have to offer. As the sport grew, so did the demands on the type of equipment needed: different lengths and shapes of ski were required for different events; a binding that would hold under new directions of shock; and softer boots. Even the length of poles and the shape of their grips were changed. Clothing became less restrictive to allow for more movement. Goggles, hats and socks changed to accommodate these adaptations. Today, all of these items have become highly specialised.

A professional freestyler needs three different types of skis—one for each event. In Ballet a short, light ski is needed that will spin when kept flat on the snow but give a good edge set to initiate aerial manoeuvres. Most ski companies make ballet skis. A fine example is the Roy Hot Pro, that features a slightly turned up tail, a flat base without a groove and strong construction to support the weight placed on their short length. The average ballet ski length should be about chin high, though it can vary according to personal preference. When just beginning, the general rule is the shorter the better but as one progresses into performing routines a little length is needed to keep the tricks smooth and flowing. The bindings should be mounted so that the middle of the boot is on the middle of the running surface of the ski or slightly back from that point. This makes for a more even spinning ski with both sides sliding equally. To have the perfect ballet ski it must be well tuned. This is done with a file and wax. Keep the edges under the boots at right angles so that the skis can still hold on the snow. From about 25 cm from the ends of the ski gently bevel the edges so that more of the angle is taken off as the end of the ski nears. This will keep the edges from catching in the snow. The final touch is a good hot wax with an iron. Remove all the wax while warm and a perfectly smooth surface will remain. The skis are now ready to "dance".

A pair of skis is also needed for the aerial discipline. Ballet skis would be too short and weak to last through many pounding landings. But at the same time an aerial ski cannot be too long because that means more weight to pull through the air. A wide ski is used, the average length used by most competitors being 170 cm. This is long and strong enough to absorb the landing without breaking the ski, and light enough not to affect the different aerial manoeuvres. It is also short enough to give the right amount of bend when going off the back or front kicker. The bindings should be placed a bit forward on the ski but not as much as with the ballet ski. The aerial ski should be prepared in the same manner as the ballet ski, but filing off less of the edge. A good wax job will ensure a smooth inrun to the ramp. Always leave the groove so that the ski will track properly.

The final discipline is the bumps. There are many opinions on how long bump skis should be. A bump ski is a very personal item because it is a reflection of the way the individual skis. Some skiers like to cruise through the moguls on 210 cm skis others like to hop around on a pair of 170 cm skis. The average length of the bump ski has varied considerably. Initially, very short lengths were popular but during the past few years longer skis have made a comeback. Today the average length is around 190 cm, but in general they are softer, to fit between the bumps with more side cut (narrower in the middle) to turn quicker. This evolution in the length of skis has created a ski that turns more quickly, with more stability than ever before. Bump skis should be given even better care than the aerial or ballet skis. Good filing of the edges and the smoothness of the running base is directly related to the quality of one's skiing. No matter how good the skier, if the edges don't hold or a slice in the base catches in the snow, the skier

won't be able to perform at his best.

A freestyler must have utmost confidence in his bindings as well as in his skis. It would be impossible to do a flip or charge down a steep bump run if the skier thought there was a chance of the binding pre-releasing. Yet it must release in a slow twisting fall in ballet, forwards if the tip digs in the snow during an uncompleted flip, or from a strong jolt received in the bumps. Freestyle puts bindings through the most demanding tests. Safety straps have always been dangerous due to the chance of a ski staying with the skier during a fall and hitting him. Ski stoppers are now used so that the ski will stop by itself. Boots have also changed, placing more emphasis on comfort while skiing. Softer flexes, easier buckle systems and lighter materials have helped bring this about. Clothes have become warmer and less restrictive as the wind tunnel look has disappeared. No longer must everything look fast. Colours and comfort are what counts.

Freestyle has brought a change to every skier. Compact skis have given the beginner an easier way to learn and the intermediate skier more confidence by making it easier to turn the skis. Through a process of trial and error, a balanced ski length has been found as well as better balanced, more precise boots for the more advanced. Products are designed specifically for skiing rather than racing—such as double lens goggles and pole grips that hold the hands without straps. Many new products have arrived on the market over the past couple of years which can be directly related to the freestyle way of skiing.

THE BUMPS

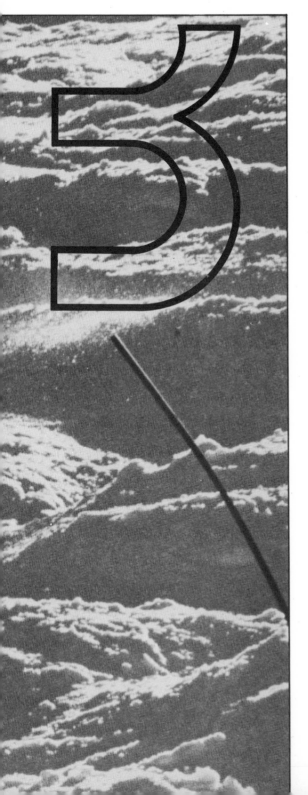

Once a skier has reached a proficient level, in most cases meaning consistent parallel turns, there are several directions in which to extend his ability. A slower skier might be happy to perfect the parallel turn with the intention of becoming a ski instructor. Another skier might choose racing as the best means to express his skiing as well as the best way to improve. Another might find satisfaction in simply skiing as many different slopes as possible. In the past ten years a new direction has come along—the bumps. The bumps, also known as moguls or munch monsters, offer the greatest challenge to any skier because of the continually varying terrain. It is a testing ground to see how quickly one can turn the skis, while keeping control at high speeds. The moguls are unforgiving. One mistake while skiing hard and the mountain will claim another victory. Skiing is a feeling of exhilaration and self-satisfaction. You know when everything is going at its best and you know when nothing connects. When skiing a steep mogul field, you know when you have made a mistake because it lets you know. The challenge of conquering a steep bump run while stretching one's ability to the very limit is the goal of the freestyle skier.

What is a freestyle bump skier?

Bumps take many different forms, as do skiers; exactly how free is the freestyle technique? Let's take a look at each one of these words, starting with "bumps". Bumps vary as much as the slopes they are found on. They can be so big that you can't see over them—or so small that they disappear after two inches of new snow; nice and round or chopped like steps; close together or far apart. Their shapes and sizes depend on many different factors: the depth of snow, its hardness or softness, which in turn is dependent on the air temperature, the steepness of the slope, who and how many people are skiing over the same area, what length of skis are being used and how long the bumps have been there since the last snowfall. Soft snow makes deep moguls, short skis create chopped, tight ones. Longer skis on easy going skiers will form round, wide moguls. The steeper the slope the quicker the bumps will form because more edge is being used to carve the turn so more snow is being dug out on each turn. This is the action that creates all bumps and keeps them growing until a snowfall fills in the troughs or a packer flattens them.

A good skier passes through the bumps no matter what their shape or size. He understands the fundamentals of good skiing. He has probably been taught these fundamentals by an instructor. There are varied techniques taught in different ski schools throughout the world, but they all come down to the same basics; knees bent forward, weight over the boots, the upper body relaxed and the mind aware. If such a skier wants to take his ability to the limit, then he is ready to be a freestyle bump skier. Many ex-alpine racers such as Suzie Corrock of the U.S., Nano Portier of France, Willy Bailey of England and Gary Holt of Australia, have made the transition from racing to competitive bump skiing with success.

Another type of skier—found in resorts throughout the world—ready for the bumps is the one who at every opportunity finds time to ski but never has the time for lessons. He might live in a ski area working nights in a bar, make beds or operate lifts. He might work or go to school in the city, spending weekends in the mountains. These self-taught thrill seekers adapt quickly to their skis and are seen speeding down all parts of the mountain until they reach the steep mogul runs, otherwise known as ''bump city''. After a crash and a couple of near wipeouts they return to other slopes to regain their self-confidence. The desire to excel and the body potential are both present but education is needed. Their own technique is not sufficient for the demands of the toughest slope on the mountain. Instruction and practice on flatter, smoother bumps will provide the key for skiing bump city.

This is true for any skier who wants to improve; but at a certain point a skier, like a baby, starts to develop his own personality. He starts skiing in a way that conforms to his body and personal style. He develops a style that is strictly his own and expresses it through his skiing. The essential body technique is there, now the mind must be trained. The body will react if the mind can send the commands quickly enough. This is freestyle in the bumps; mind over matter. It is a personal confrontation, man against himself with moguls, snow and skis as the medium. A victory is scored every time a bumper arrives at the bottom of bump city, knowing that he has turned as quickly, skied as fast, and jumped as high as his ability allows, while keeping constant control.

Ten years ago when freestyle was just beginning, and was known more as hot dogging, it was approached differently. Freestyle skiing was simply getting down the hill in the craziest, most spectacular way imaginable. In mogul competition falls and good recoveries scored as high as did crazy turns, flips off the poles and even ballet manoeuvres. As with everything, the mogul event has changed a lot since then, to the point where some people would say it could hardly be called free.

Turns, control, air are all part of a perfect bump run. Carved turns are necessary to keep the skis under control. In other words, an edge set must be made so that the ski digs into the snow. A sliding ski will not give a quick response.

Skiing bump city is one thing but playing on its surface, by adding spreads, daffies, helicopters and other jumps is quite another. These require utmost confidence and a desire to show the mountain who is in control. But be careful. A miscalculated jump can be disastrous; leaving skis, poles and perhaps bits of the skier all over the side of the hill. As if all of this is not enough, one final ingredient must be added to separate the men from the boys, and that is speed. To find out what a difference speed makes time yourself while skiing as fast as possible down your favourite bump run, not forgetting turns, air and especially control. Find a run that takes about twenty seconds. Take three readings and then try to beat the fastest time by two seconds. Did you still have control and were you able to get any air?

Save this experience until the other aspects of skiing come naturally. The fundamentals must be learned first. Mogul skiing is an advanced technique because a sensitivity or feeling for the skis must be acquired. This comes with ski mileage and improved technique. The fundamentals are not difficult to understand but actually ''putting it to work'' takes patience and practice. How many times has it been said, ''I know what I have to do it's just that my skis don't''. Here are several pointers that will help your skis find out what they have to do to improve your bump skiing.

SKIS APART Too many skiers concentrate on locking their skis together in a closed or parallel stance. This creates several problems. It takes the mind off more important points. It makes for a less secure stance, because more balance is obtained when the feet are wider apart. The wide stance also helps when a quick recovery is needed. A closed stance also causes skiers to ski with their hips using both skis as one instead of working them independently. Only when the weight is transferred from one ski to the other can edge control work to make a proper turn. This is not to say that skiing with the skis together is wrong. As long as the turns are parallel, let the skis find their natural position whether apart or together. As mileage is accumulated the skis will naturally come closer, but when the conditions get rough let them find the most stable position.

INDEPENDENT EDGE CONTROL A correct advanced turn is a carved turn using the entire length of the ski. Sliding on both skis is fine if nothing steeper than the beginners slope is to be attempted. But if one desires to descend to the more difficult areas, with control, the skier must learn to work his skis independently of each other so as to get the edge control necessary for a carved turn. The edge of the outside ski carves the turn by keeping the knees pressed forward and into the hill while driving the skis around by applying pressure on the balls of the feet. Once the turn has been completed the weight is transferred to the other ski and it repeats the same movement. By having the skis working independently, underneath the body, control can be maintained under any condition.

KNEES FORWARD The steepness of the hill and the speed of the skier will always be a force pulling the body backwards. One must continuously push forwards to keep the body and knees over the boots and skis. If the weight of the skier is on the tails of the skis maximum control is lost. Knees must also be bent forward so that pressure can be applied to the edge of the skis. While standing straight, with or without skis, try to push the knees to one side or the other. Now, bend the knees forward over the toes and try it again. The turning power is delivered from the knees and they must stay bent and loose.

UPPER BODY AND HIPS SQUARE DOWN THE HILL Mogul skiing is performed down the fall line. The body from the hips up should always be facing down the hill with the skis turning and checking underneath; the idea being that the upper body interferes as little as possible while the legs, knees and skis do the work. If the body sits backwards or the hips twist to one side the lower body is limited in what it can do.

A good skier will be noticed on the hill by the manner in which his body remains calm while skiing quickly over the bumpiest terrain. His body won't be standing erect but loose, with legs bent so bumps are absorbed rather than bounced off.

ARMS AND HEAD STILL Some skiers come down the hill flapping their arms as though attempting to fly, their heads moving back and forth thinking they are making radical turns only to be told at the bottom that they had skied straight the whole time. Once again; everything must be kept still. The less upper body movement the more the legs are left unhindered to do their job. The arms should be kept in front of the body to help it stay forward, and are used to anticipate and prepare for a turn with a pole plant that is no more than a wrist action. The head should be looking straight down the hill analysing where the skis are heading.

BODY AND MIND RELAXED A stiff skier will have a rough time skiing any slope. A good night's sleep, being fit, loosening up before attacking the more difficult runs, and a peaceful mind all help in skiing the bumps. Letting yourself flow with the terrain, the skis finding their own path as the rest of the body fixes to the pattern, help in conquering bump city. Don't let yourself be psyched out but take a couple of easy runs to get the feel and then see if you can "go for it".

In spite of the set conditions of bump skiing it is still free. You can choose your own path and the speed at which you want to ski it. Let yourself go and find your own potential. This has been happening since the beginning of skiing. The major developments over the years have been in the directions of greater speed and attainment of more air. There is no time to add the extra showmanship of a ballet trick or pole flip while racing down a 30 degree slope full of munch monsters. It is full-on skiing.

BUMP SEQUENCE

1 As the snow shoots out from under the outside ski a carved turn is being finished as the outside pole anticipates the next turn. The legs are strongly angulated (bent) so that pressure is exerted on the edge of the skis. The upper body is facing square down the hill.

2 The upper body retains its position as the unweighted skis pass underneath. The planted pole is now being withdrawn as the other comes forward.

3 The skis are carving against a bump. Thus the contours of the hill are being used to the advantage of the skier. Not as much pressure or angulation is needed. Again the body is aimed down the hill and the pole is ready to initiate the next turn.

4 As the bumps get closer a quicker turn is needed.

5 Coming head-on into a mogul the skis spread for more balance as the body absorbs the shock by having the legs come right up into it. As the boots pass over the top of the bump the highest point is used to initiate the next turn by pivoting the skis with the knees.

6 Keeping in the troughs or valleys of the moguls the body keeps its low profile and the skis give a strong edge set.

7 Skiing straight into the bump, instead of absorbing it, an extension is made.

8 Flying into the air a daffy is performed.

9 Skis come together for a smooth landing.

10 An edge set is quickly made to bring the flying skis under control and the run is continued.

BALLET

Ballet skiing on snow is what figure skating is on ice. Identical end results are sought, whether on skis or skates. An experienced ballet skier, like an expert figure skater, seeks difficult tricks and choreographed routines, put together in a symphony of smoothness and originality. The hours spent on practising individual tricks, selecting the right music and adding it all together to perform a self produced show is incredible. Talent—but mostly practice and dedication—separate the best from the good. But ballet skiing is much more than the task of producing a winning routine. It is fun. Fun for anyone who wants to give it a try. Just as a person who has only been ice skating a couple of times might try to lift up one leg or skate backwards, a novice skier can try the same things on skis. There are tricks demonstrated here that anybody can attempt; and if nothing more than a laugh is gained from the experience it is worth it. Ballet skiing is for anyone who wants to try something new. There is such a wealth of tricks, many that are found in the following pages, that there is something for everyone.

Ballet skiing can be the fun of attempting a couple of tricks or the seriousness of programming a routine. Amateur as well as professional competitions have given everyone a chance to demonstrate their capabilities. Throughout the world freestyle ballet classes have attracted students of all ages as well as those who were simply curious to see what it was all about. It should be made clear that all freestyle disciplines, including ballet, when progressed to an advanced level, are for good parallel skiers who are physically fit. A lot of tension and strain is placed on all parts of the body; especially the knees as they must twist in so many directions and to such extremes. When learning new tricks falls must be expected; but if the proper progression is followed, and one does not over extend one's self, they can be kept to a minimum. Not only does ballet teach tricks that most people would think impossible but it also helps one's every day skiing because of the necessary mastery of change of balance and the different pressures and motions used to turn the skis.

This section contains descriptions of many different tricks. There are enough tricks here for one

to either sample some of the easier ones or to provide something stimulating for the more advanced student. There are other tricks—some that haven't been invented yet—that will always provide something new and challenging. These can be learnt by watching other skiers; or perhaps you might invent a movement of your own. Every new season sees advances in the art of ballet skiing, with new and more difficult tricks that attest to the freestyler's desire for progress and originality. The constant variation of putting together old tricks also demonstrates this. There are no set rules or methods for combining tricks. Whatever looks and feels best to the individual can be done. The following descriptions set out what is believed to be the easiest way of learning a given trick. Try the methods suggested here first but if any other way is found don't be afraid to try it.

Basic ballet can be divided into three motions: skiing on the inside ski, rotations or spins, and crossing one ski over the other. By learning these fundamental movements and understanding the technique of the three basic tricks—skiing on the inside ski, 360 degree spins on both skis and a crossover—it will be easier to understand and execute the more difficult tricks that follow. As in all freestyle disciplines one must constantly concentrate on what the skis are doing. Even when one has a trick so wired that it's never missed, attention must still be given to the smaller details so that it is done perfectly. When watching an experienced ballet skier, skis appear to be on back to front, legs seem to tangle and untangle every ten feet and even the poles seem to get lost during elaborate displays of an assortment of tricks. But once a spectrum of the basic tricks is learned, an understanding of the pressures, twists and placings of skis and legs, a total picture of the ballet process emerges. The progression into more advanced ballet is a continuation of what has already been learned. A skier can take ballet as far as desired. Some people want to learn a couple of tricks to add a further dimension to their skiing, while others see ballet as a whole new way of skiing.

The ballet section has been divided into four parts so that a learning progression can be followed. The first section, showing twenty different basic ballet tricks, starts with the proper ballet stance followed by three basic tricks. These manoeuvres demonstrate most of the motions that will be needed to execute the tricks that follow. The second section deals with a few basic gymnastic manoeuvres. These are especially useful on bad days when visibility is poor and skiing is pretty much out of the question. These stunts involve a lot of rolling on and in the snow, so dress accordingly. It can get wet. Tricks using the ski poles are demonstrated in the third section. When done properly a pole trick adds a lot of flair to a routine because of the height that can be obtained. The basic tip roll is exciting enough by itself let alone all of the tricks that progress from it. Advanced ballet, shown in the fourth section, is mostly aerial spins progressing from an Aerial 360; otherwise known as a helicopter or heli. These tricks create real excitement because of their fast action and difficulty.

Ballet tricks are best performed on a smooth, gentle slope where the snow is dry and well packed. These conditions provide a perfect stage for ballet, one that is free of obstacles that might catch a ski, or transitions that might change the tempo of the ballet run. When the snow is dry it has the same texture over the whole slope, helping the smoothness and consistency of the run, and providing a surface that is hard enough for the skis to stay on the top, while at the same time soft enough to cushion a fall. Unfortunately conditions are not always so ideal. New tricks should be learnt when the conditions are best, but a good ballet skier should be able to perform on just about any surface.

As in all sports, ballet is best learnt from an instructor. Small details that cause big problems can be spotted and corrected by someone with teaching experience. But the ballet skiers who are now teaching had to learn without today's knowledge. The most difficult part of the sport is developing new and original tricks. Seven years ago there were only a few basic tricks and from then on it was up to one's own originality. The ballet tricks that are described in the following pages will provide a base. They can be learned independently or in conjunction with an instructor. When using the book, read the trick right through to get an overall picture of what is happening, then read it a second time to pick out the particulars. If problems persist, turn to the *Helpful Hints (HH)* section at the end of each trick. If it still won't come together, question another ballet skier on the hill or find an instructor.

The best way to understand a trick is to practise without skis before going on to the snow. Get a feeling of what is happening to all the parts of the body so that when it is done with skis the motions happen naturally and concentration can be focused on the skis. With non spinning tricks, the next step is to practise with the skis while in a stationary position. Feel how the skis affect the different movements. When the mind understands what must be done then the body is ready. Without following the proper progression into a trick the learning process can be frustrating and slow. Try to progress into different tricks. Don't try one that is too advanced. Take a trick apart and try various aspects of it, then combine those parts to execute the whole trick. As you are perfecting old manoeuvres, learn new ones. Develop a combination of tricks as soon as possible so that a personalised routine can be started. As new tricks are acquired add them together in a flowing, linked fashion to improve the routine. A flawless, easy routine is preferred to one with difficult but poorly executed tricks. Do the tricks that feel good to you and let your own personality show through. Let it all flow together gracefully and controlled. Individual ballet tricks are not difficult to learn. Perfecting them and creating a routine is not so easy. But no matter how far one gets into ballet an attempt at the sport will open up a new world full of possibilities most skiers believe are for a privileged few.

BASIC BALLET STANCE

In ballet a stance is required which not only looks good but also provides balance and control and will act as a transition between tricks. This basic stance is shown here with skis slightly apart, legs pushed gently forward, the body held upright with the hands held high in front of the body, and the head held up looking forward. Almost all tricks can be started from this position. By having the legs slightly bent the skier has more control over his skis whilst maintaining a more elegant stance. To keep this stance and the body erect the head must be held up. Most learners tend to look at their skis, which causes the waist to bend and creates bad habits—as well as making the manoeuvres more difficult. The hands should be held forward for balance and also for making their own movements. Once a routine has been learnt, the usage of hands and poles becomes an integral part of the overall effect. An upright ballet stance gives more stature to the skier and will make any routine, whether basic or advanced, look good. A smile also makes a run look more relaxed and elegant. The early ballet runs of Wayne Wong are classic examples of a proper stance and a big smile.

2o basic tricks

SKI ON THE INSIDE SKI

When learning to ski a student is taught to weight the outside turning ski. This enables pressure to be put on that ski and give it the power to turn. As he progresses more advanced techniques are learned but the weight remains mostly on the outside ski. In ballet however one must be prepared to ski on either ski—frontwards, backwards, or sideways. Skiing on the inside ski is the first step in changing this normal pattern and breaking into the world of ballet. This trick can be done anywhere with any length of ski but it is best to keep to flatter slopes—especially for the first few attempts.

Technique

1 Ski across the hill at a fairly good speed in the ballet stance.

2 Prepare to jump off the uphill ski by bending the knees and applying the weight to that ski. The body is still facing across the hill.

3 A slight jump has been made changing the edge of the lower or inside ski. The initiation step of the turn has been made and the body is now facing downhill with the weight on the inside ski.

4–7 The body position remains forward with pressure towards the front of the foot. By having started the turn properly, keeping the inside ski fairly flat on the snow and guiding the ski around as in a normal turn, the skis will come all the way around.

Helpful Hints

● Starting the turn a slight jump should be made when learning so that the edge of the downhill ski changes from the uphill side to the inside edge. If this isn't done the skis will keep going straight instead of turning. To prepare for this manoeuvre do an uphill inside christy. Turn up the hill on the uphill ski so that a smaller turn is made.

● During the turn the body must be kept forward and the knees bent to give control to the skis.

This is one of the basic manoeuvres. Understanding the principles here will help make all the "on snow spinning" tricks easier. At first it helps to do the 360° spin with a wide stance so that better balance is obtained. As you progress bring the skis closer together. Once the 360° spin is mastered in both directions don't stop there but go around two or three times. Get a feeling for keeping the skis flat on the snow while making them go around. Spotting can also be learnt while doing two ski spins.

Technique

1 Go straight down the hill, pick up a bit of speed and start a normal turn, edging only slightly.

2 As you start to face uphill push your weight forward so that the tips of the skis catch and the tails come around.

3 You are now facing uphill and must bring the skis around another 180 degrees. The momentum is usually not enough to continue the spin so pressure must be applied to the tails of the skis by leaning back and then pulling the knees, legs and skis around until

4 the 360° is complete. To continue spinning, push the knees forward, bring the tails around and do another 360° as before.

Helpful Hints

• Don't edge too much when starting the spin or it will come to an abrupt halt. The skis must remain flat on the snow and the body square over the skis.

• Don't turn the skis by pivoting them or twisting the feet. The skis will only get a portion of the way around but never the whole circle. Get the feeling of turning the skis by rocking back and forth over the boots, letting the knees guide the skis around.

CROSSOVER

Also known as a stepover this classic ballet trick has been around for many years. The name states what must be done; if the proper technique is followed it is easily mastered, otherwise the crossover can be a real leg tangler. That is why short skis and several stationary attempts are recommended before doing it on the move. Before going up the hill find a flat area and follow the technique while standing still. Read the (*HH*) closely.

Technique

1 Starting in the ballet stance the downhill leg is brought slightly backwards.

2 A good kick sends the ski high over the other.

3 The crossed over ski is placed on the snow, aiming up the hill, so that the tips of the skis are about a foot apart.

4 At this stage the poles can be used for balance as the upper body rocks forward on the ski that has just been placed on the snow. This enables the retracting leg to remain straight as it is brought back. The important step here is to lift the ski tip towards the outside instead of pulling the ski straight back. If this is not properly executed the ski tip will catch in the snow causing loss of balance or a fall.

5 The ski is brought high behind the body.

6 The foot is then pivoted so that the ski is aimed up the hill. The leg remains straight.

7 As the upper body is straightened the leg comes down.

8 The trick is completed by returning to the proper ballet stance.

Helpful Hints

● When placing the crossed over ski on the snow don't place it close to the other. This will cause loss of balance and there is a good chance of catching an edge. It also makes it hard to bring the other ski back to its normal position.

● Don't remain in crossed over position any longer than it takes to put one ski down and lift the other one up. It is a precarious stance when skis are crossed over and weight is on both skis.

● Keep an upright stance except when bringing the ski around behind you.

● When placing the crossed over ski on the snow guide its direction by placing the weight forward on it or the ski will tend to turn up the hill.

In 1929 Dr Reuel published a book called *New Possibilities In Skiing* in which he presented the Reuel Christy for the first time. He was so far ahead of his time that when his trick turned up again the spelling of its name had changed. The Royal Turn is not difficult, although it takes much more balance than simply skiing on the inside ski. It is an easy trick to learn because as one improves skiing on the inside ski, the outside ski must be lifted higher and higher and soon the Royal position is reached.

Technique

1 As in all inside ski turns the problem of initiation must be mastered. It is important to hop on to the downhill ski which will become the inside ski in the turn. As this is mastered the "pop" will decrease to a more subtle change.

2–4 Once the turn has commenced the outside ski is raised as high as possible. The upper body can be upright or bent forward. The arms are held out to the sides and the head up. The turning motion of the ski is controlled by keeping the weight forward on the ball of the foot, keeping the ski flat and sliding.

Helpful Hints

• If there are any problems with the Royal Turn review the steps of skiing on the inside ski.

ONE SKI 360° SPIN

This is a difficult trick because it combines the initiation step used when skiing on the inside ski, the rocking motion of the 360° spin and an upper body rotation. The movements are easy to execute without skis and can be practised anywhere. Try it and see what must be done to get the body to spin on one foot. Once the skis are on do this trick by first skiing across the hill and spinning up the hill. The same movements are used when doing it in the fall line.

Technique

1 Head down the hill with the upper body turned slightly away from the spinning direction. The inside arm is ready as if to make a normal turn.

2 The weight is pushed on to the inside ski and the upper body and outside arm come around to start the spin.

3–5 If the ski is kept flat it will keep spinning. The rotation can be sped up by pivoting the ski, as done in the 360° spin on two skis, but the main force of the spin must come from the initial thrust.

6 When the 360 degrees is reached the spin can be stopped by bringing the lifted ski on to the snow.

Helpful Hints

● To get the feeling of starting the spin try it often without skis.

● Use the arms to get the spin going and then lift the outside ski—don't lift the ski first and then try the spin.

● To keep the skis spinning they must be kept flat on the snow. Any edge will stop them. A straight upper body and knees bent stance will help this.

OUTRIGGER

As far back as 1956 an instructor named Doug Pfeiffer started a freestyle school which he called the School of Exotic Skiing. The trick that he made popular and which is still often used today, though rarely seen in top competition, is named the outrigger—for reasons that are apparent as soon as the position is observed. In Germany it is called the "Fuzzy Schwung" meaning "Fuzzy's Turn", named after the popular and long time freestyler Heinz "Fuzzy" Garhammer who was instrumental in getting freestyle going in Europe.

Technique

1 To get into the outrigger position, a slight jump or step is made to bring the weight to the inside ski.

2 As the turn is made the body sinks lower.

3–5 The body remains low with the weight forward, hands held out to the sides and the outside leg extended.

Helpful Hints

● Keep the body forward over the knee so that control can be kept over the skis and also to keep from sitting in the snow.

● The ski that is the outrigger should not have its base or edges touching the snow. Place the knee of the outstretched leg close to the snow to keep the edge out of the snow.

● Before trying the outrigger in a turn it is best to understand the position while stationary, either with skis or without. Stand on a flat area and extend one leg while keeping all the weight on the other. Keep the body and weight well forward while bending as low as possible as shown in steps 3–5. This is the position that is maintained throughout the turn.

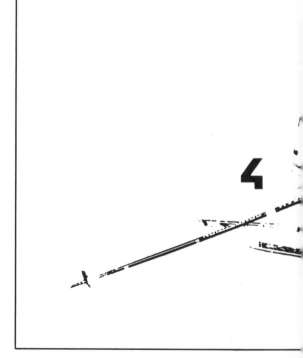

The name speaks for itself. Start the spin by dragging the tip of one ski in the snow and continue spinning 360 degrees. A tip drag 360 is easy because such little effort is required to do the trick. When the tip is placed properly in the snow to initiate the spin the rest happens automatically.

Technique

1 Head down the hill at a reasonable speed and lift one of the skis slightly off the snow. Turn the ski that is off the snow until it is at right angles to the other ski and so that one boot is behind the other. At this point the extended ski is placed in the snow so that the tip catches while the surface ski remains as flat as possible.

2 By catching the tip in the snow the body rotates to catch up to it.

3 As the sliding ski spins it will become parallel with the ski that was initially placed to the side.

4 More than half the turn has been made; the skis are now parallel and weight is equally distributed.

5 If the skis are kept flat on the snow the momentum created from catching the tip will bring the skis all the way around.

Helpful Hints

• Bring the ski that starts the spin well behind the body before placing the tip in the snow. This will give much more momentum.

• Don't bend at the waist but keep the body erect.

• The best way to try the tip drag 360 for the first time is to traverse the slope using the uphill ski to initiate the spin. This is easier than heading straight down the hill.

REVERSE CROSSOVER

The reverse crossover is the crossover done from back to front. Although the movements are the same this trick is much more difficult because each step is so critical. The reverse crossover should be tried many times in a stationary position before doing it while skiing. When learning, always begin with the uphill ski. This is very important because it makes the manoeuvre much easier to complete. Once it has been mastered the reverse crossover can be added in a spin or a turn.

Technique

1 Ski slowly across the hill in the ballet stance.

2 Lean forward and bring the uphill ski behind the body; not by pulling it straight back but by rotating the ski tip up the hill. Use the poles for balance if necessary and maintain a low speed when learning this trick.

3 Once the ski is behind the body the most crucial step begins. From here the foot must be twisted so that the ski is pointing straight down the hill.

4 If this is done, and the ski tip is kept to the side, it will easily come parallel to the other. If not the ski tip will catch in the snow and the trick will have an abrupt finish.

5–6 Once the ski hits the snow it is important to quickly lift up what is now the uphill ski. The crossed over position is dangerous when weight is placed on both skis because both skis are edging on the inside and will cross over each other.

7 Return to the ballet stance.

Helpful Hints

● The biggest problem is always in the beginning when bringing the uphill ski around and behind the other. Several movements help: bend forward at the waist to let the leg lift higher; keep the extended leg straight; pivot the foot 180 degrees before bringing the leg down.

● Practise on a slope while not skiing.

● Once the skis are crossed over separate them quickly.

● Always start with the uphill ski.

1

2

3

CHARLESTON

This ballet step, which looks just like the dance step of the same name, consists simply of short connecting turns on the inside ski while kicking up the outside ski. Even though it appears simple it is more easily done on the dance floor than on the slope. The Charleston is best practised on a very gentle slope. Face down the hill with skis in a slight snow plough. Place the poles in front of you to keep from sliding forwards. Jump up and place the left ski where the right had been and then place the right where the left was. Get a rhythm going and then do it while skiing. The only difference while in motion is that when the ski lands on the snow, a slight heel thrust must be exerted to control the speed.

Technique

1 The weight is on the left ski, the right is in the air.

2 A jump has been made—both skis are in the air.

3 Weight comes down on the right ski as the left gets kicked in the air.

4–5 Continue the same movements using the arms to help balance.

Helpful Hints

● Get a rhythm going as though dancing.

● Start with wide turns on the inside ski making them smaller and smaller until the Charleston is happening.

MERMAID

This is not a difficult trick but it does take a sense of balance to maintain the position. The Mermaid is a good transitional trick and can add grace to any routine. A variation can be effected by skiing down the hill, controlling the speed by applying pressure to the tip of the trailing ski.

Technique

1 While skiing across the hill lift either ski.

2 Place the tip of the ski in the snow directly behind you. The more pressure applied to the tip the more braking there will be.

3 At this point arch the body and bring the head back.

Helpful Hints

● As the back is arched dig the tip of the upright ski into the snow and keep enough pressure on it so that the ski is felt strongly in the back. This pressure and the outstretched hands will help to keep the ski from wavering.

JAVELIN TURN

(*Not pictured*)

Here is another one of the original ballet tricks. It is so easy that many skiers try to add something that is not there and become confused. A parallel skier should be able to do the Javelin Turn on his first go.

Technique

Ski across the hill and start a normal parallel turn. The weight should be totally on the outside ski. As the turn progresses, the inside ski twists over the outside ski. Try to twist it as far as possible. This can also be done while traversing.

Helpful Hints

● Keep the weight squarely over the turning ski so that control is maintained during the turn.

● The more the ski is twisted over the top of the other the better the trick looks.

SHEA GUY

It takes a lot of practice but mainly a pair of rubber legs to execute the trick made popular by Mike Shea, American all around freestyle star. It can be performed across the hill or in turns—the turns being the most difficult. Because of the extreme twisting of the legs the Shea Guy should not be practised for long periods of time. Loosen up the legs by doing a Shea Guy in a stationary position before trying it on the move.

Technique

1 Ski across the hill, bring the uphill ski around behind you so that it is parallel with the other only facing in the opposite direction. This is the Shea Guy position.

2 To turn apply weight to the ski that is headed forwards and push the tail of the outside ski further around.

3 Use the inside ski for balance but keep an edge on the outside ski so that the position can be maintained.

4 From here the position can be changed or a turn in the opposite direction can be made.

Helpful Hints

● Because people are built differently, not everyone can do the Shea Guy. Test your flexibility by attempting to stand in this position on the flat. If the knees start hurting it is best to move on to other tricks.

● If the position can be maintained keep pressure on the forward heading ski while skiing. Let the other follow.

5

The name indicates what must be done. One ski must jump over the other. One variation called the Flying Royal calls for the uphill ski to jump over the downhill ski, keeping the same direction. Another variation is shown with the Jump Over Twist. There are others too. It just takes a bit of imagination.

Technique

1 Start by placing the skis horizontally to the slope, the upper body facing down the hill with the downhill pole planted to the side of the body.

2 The uphill ski starts twisting around the downhill boot. At the same time the upper body is also twisting. From here, a jump is made as a result of the downhill leg projecting the body down the hill.

3 By turning the body and ski while in the air a correct landing will be made with the ski heading in the opposite direction and (what was) the downhill ski ending behind, tip in the snow.

4 Jump overs can be connected by dropping the ski that is in the air below the body.

5 At this point pick up what is now the uphill ski and project it over the other ski. This can be continued until either there is no more slope or you end up in a knot.

Helpful Hints

● Go for it. There is no half way point with a jump over. Holding back will only cause one ski to land on top of the other instead of making the 180 degrees.

● When performing a Jump Over series, otherwise known as a Tornado, keep the skis horizontal to the slope by jumping and bringing the skis to the correct position.

2

The initial steps are the same as in the Jump Over but at step three a new movement is added.

Technique

1 Instead of dropping the uphill ski rock forward on the surface ski, and by moving the weight forwards on to the balls of the feet pivot the ski 180 degrees. While turning let the other ski come down on the snow.

2 The skis end up parallel and the Jump Over Twist can be started again.

Helpful Hints

● This is a good trick to practise the motion of pivoting the ski. It will be used with other tricks.

● Rocking the skis forward will enable the ends of the skis to come around. If this is not done the edges will catch.

The Outrigger 360 combines several basic manoeuvres: skiing on the inside ski, the Outrigger position, and a 360 Spin. Top ballet freestyler Wayne Wong stopped the crowds by doing two consecutive Outrigger 360s back in 1971. Today the trick is not seen much in competition but is still fun.

Technique

1 Start in an Outrigger position with the weight on the inside ski and rotate the upper body in preparation for the initiation of the spin.

2 Continue turning the ski as explained in a normal Outrigger turn.

3 The upper body has initiated the spin by rotating the arms and body into the turn. Weight is kept forward on the inside ski.

4–5 The outside ski is completely unweighted while the surface ski is kept as flat as possible so that it will continue to spin.

6 As the turn reaches completion, weight is placed on the outside ski to stop the momentum.

7 A lower stance is assumed.

Helpful Hints

● Choose a very smooth surface when learning this trick. Spinning is not easy while in a crouched position.

● If problems persist review the Turn On The Inside Ski and the Outrigger position.

ROYAL 360

The Royal 360 is executed exactly as the One Ski 360 Spin except the outside ski is lifted as high as possible. Initiate the spin with the upper body and let a flat ski and slight rocking motion keep the skis spinning. Huia Irwin, 1977 New Zealand and Australian Freestyle Champion, demonstrates a variation on the normal Royal 360. Instead of going into the spin forwards and letting the arms start the turn, Huia initiates the turn with her leg, going backwards into the spin.

Technique

1 A wedge, or snowplough, prepares for the start of the spin.

2 From here the leg that will be held up during the spin is lifted up and brought around behind the other. This, along with the rotation of the arms and body, starts the momentum for the spin.

3–6 The body is kept spinning by a slight forwards and backwards motion while the ski remains as flat as possible, the lifted ski being held as high as possible.

Helpful Hints

• Practise the One Ski 360 and progress into the Royal 360 by trying to lift the outside ski higher each time.

• Use the pole for balance if necessary.

• The Royal 360 is not as easy as it looks because the surface ski must be kept flat on the snow in order to keep it spinning. This is difficult when in the Royal position.

The Leg Breaker is not as formidable as it sounds but it does put unusual stress on the knees. When done quickly there is less stress, so go into the trick knowing what must be done. Once learned the Leg Breaker series is a very flamboyant manoeuvre.

Technique

1 Stand across the hill and place the tip of the downhill ski next to the tail of the uphill ski.

2 Keeping the tip in the snow, the ski is directed downhill until it is parallel to the other, only facing in the opposite direction. This is a strenuous twisting position and should not be held for long.

3 Quickly lift the uphill ski, keeping the tail on the snow. This will relieve the pressure on the knees. The ski that is in the air is now brought over the other ski. Pivot the leg so that the skis remain parallel, even though headed in opposite directions.

4 When the ski arrives on the snow, the other will follow behind and another Leg Breaker can be started.

Helpful Hints

• Keep the skis parallel whenever they are on the snow so that they remain horizontal to the slope.

• Know what must be done before attempting the Leg Breaker so that a pause isn't needed in the middle of the trick.

4

CROSS TWIST

This trick is very useful in learning how to pivot the surface ski. Many more advanced tricks use this same movement. The Cross Twist is started by crossing the downhill ski over the uphill one.

Technique

1 Come into the Crossover position.

2 Put the weight on the ski that has just been crossed over, lean well forward and lift the other ski so that it doesn't get in the way.

3 By leaning forward on to the ball of the foot the ski will pivot more easily, especially if kept flat on the snow. Let the other ski follow.

4 Once half the spin has been made the skis come together.

5 The rest of the spin is made by the momentum created in the beginning when the foot was pivoted. If the momentum is not enough, lean backwards and bring the tips around as demonstrated in a 360 spin on two skis.

6 Return to ballet stance.

Helpful Hints

● Rock forward and keep a flat ski to complete the trick smoothly.

3

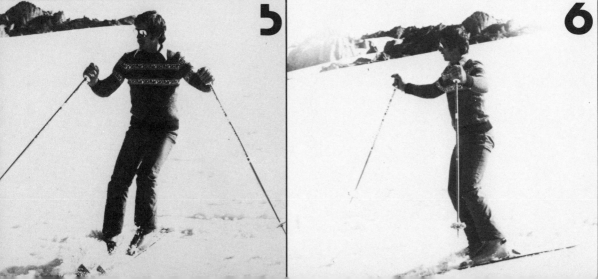

5

6

7

Once a Cross Twist is perfected the motions in this trick are more easily understood. This is a beautiful, graceful trick but fairly intricate because both skis make separate movements. It is further complicated when done without poles, as demonstrated here by Katy Buckland, 1976 Australian Ballet Champion.

Technique

1 Ski across the hill, lift the downhill ski and keep the weight well forward on the ski that remains on the snow.

2 As the surface ski is pivoted, so that the tail passes underneath the lifted ski, the ski in the air is being turned in the opposite direction.

3 The aerial ski comes in behind the other.

4 When 180 degree has been completed, the skis are parallel and crossed over with the weight on the uphill ski.

5 The weight now transfers from that ski to the other. This ski controls the direction of the skier. To make a smooth transition ski a bit in this position before jumping out.

6 The uphill ski is now jumped over the other.

7 The skier skis on to the next trick.

Helpful Hints

● Stand in Crossover position as shown in step (5) and practise jumping out as shown in step (6). This will help when trying the lead on to Crossover 360.

The last of the basic ballet tricks is not so basic. A knowledge of the previous tricks will certainly help understand the mechanics, and when learning it is best to traverse the slope, crossing the uphill ski over the downhill ski. This reduces the distance required to spin before jumping out. This is a good trick to learn in both directions as well as straight down the hill. But when learning choose the direction best suited for yourself. Some skiers will find it easier to cross the left ski over the right rather than as demonstrated here.

Technique

1 Cross one ski over the other by lifting the ski high.

2 Angle it so that the tail is on one side of the surface ski and the tip on the other. This is a crossover position.

3 With the ski that is on the top, pressure is applied quickly to the tip by leaning in its direction. This catching of the tip in the snow is the force that starts the ski spinning.

4 To keep them spinning weight must be kept on the middle of the surface ski. If the ski is kept flat 180 degrees of the spin will be completed.

5 The ski on the top must be jumped over and around as in the Leg Breaker with 180 Degree Pivot.

6 The skier has now spun 360 degrees and the Crossover 360 is complete.

Helpful Hints

● Starting the manoeuvre must be done by a quick application of pressure from the ski tip in the snow; not by trying to pivot the surface ski. If too little pressure is applied there will not be enough momentum to complete the spin. If too much is applied the edge of the lower ski catches and the spin will stop.

● After applying pressure to the ski return quickly to an upright stance so that the surface ski is flat on the snow.

● Once the spin has begun the proper moment must be anticipated before jumping out. When the moment comes the ski, led by the arms and upper body, must be pivoted 180 degrees.

Getting into the Snow

Basic tumbling tricks were a common sight during the first few years of freestyle competition. The winters of 1974 and 1975 saw fewer acrobatic tricks, as skiers were aiming for a smoother, more graceful routine and placing more emphasis on skiing to music. The ballet circuit has become more competitive during the years and more flair is needed to win. Advanced tumbling manoeuvres, such as Walkovers and Pole Flips, when choreographed into a synchronised routine, offer a combination of excitement and strength. Five basic tumbling tricks are described in this section. These manoeuvres are especially fun when visibility is nil, there is not much snow, or the lift wait is an hour long. Be prepared to get damp as the snow has a way of finding any opening in a ski suit. All these tricks can be perfected first without skis, except for the worm turn.

WORM TURN

When first attempted one quickly understands where this trick gets its name from. It is never used in competition today but remains as a symbol to the first crazy days of freestyle, when anything was tried. It is still a great trick during demonstrations and always grabs the spectators' attention. Although the movements are easy, the timing is harder than it looks.

Technique

1 Go slowly, and head straight down the hill. Later more speed can be added.

2 Sit on the back of the skis, lie straight back with the arms extended behind you.

3 Look up the hill, keeping the arms extended. Start to roll over.

4 As you roll over keep the ends of the skis tight against your back. The roll must be done quickly so that speed is not lost.

5 Once the roll has been completed the skis will be heading down the fall line if they were held continuously against the back.

6 If done properly the skier will return to the position of sitting on the tails of the skis, and all that is left to do is to stand up.

Helpful Hints

● Lie completely on the tail of the skis before rolling.

● Keep the skis against your back while rolling otherwise they will not end up facing straight down the hill.

● Do the movements to the Worm Turn several times in a stationary position on a flat surface before going for it.

FRONT ROLL

The Front Roll can be done from an Outrigger position while skiing straight down the hill, or a number of other ways. The best method for learning the proper technique is as follows.

Technique

1 Face straight down the hill with skis facing opposite directions. Place the hands slightly in front of the body.

2 Fall forwards on to your hands to absorb the fall and tuck your head in so that you will roll off the top of your back.

3 As you are rolling over uncross the skis and twist them gently to the side.

4 This twisting motion keeps the tails from going straight into the snow and lets the skis land parallel to each other.

5 From that position you can quickly stand up.

Helpful Hints

● Absorb the initial shock with the hands.

● Hold the poles out to the side so they don't interfere with the movements.

● Let one leg come well forward of the other so that the skis don't catch.

BARREL ROLL

Technique

1 Assume a hunched over position with the skis placed across the fall line, arms slightly out and feet together.

2 Fall sideways (downhill) and retain the hunched over position. Brace the fall by rolling along the length of the arm and shoulder.

3 The momentum created by the steepness of the slope will bring the skier back to his feet if the proper position is maintained.

Helpful Hints

• Don't put the hand out to absorb the fall, but use the length of the arm.

• When using poles, keep them as shown in the picture.

HEAD STAND

The head stand like the Hand Stand is sometimes used at the beginning or end of a routine, though rarely these days. It is still a fun trick to attempt and useful for keeping the head cool on hot days.

Technique

1 Find a nice spot for the head and place the ski tips uphill, keeping the skis apart for a more stable position. Place the hands slightly uphill and apart.

2 Lift the skis up slowly, keeping balance with the arms and hands.

3 Get the legs straight and the skis parallel and hang in there. To get down drop backwards, landing on the skis and ski away.

Helpful Hints

● Have someone balance your skis for you while the final position is reached if it can't be done alone.

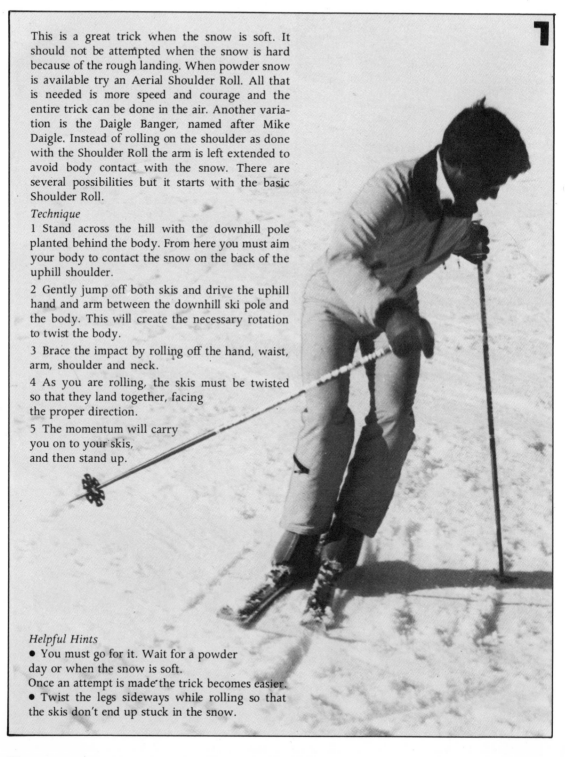

This is a great trick when the snow is soft. It should not be attempted when the snow is hard because of the rough landing. When powder snow is available try an Aerial Shoulder Roll. All that is needed is more speed and courage and the entire trick can be done in the air. Another variation is the Daigle Banger, named after Mike Daigle. Instead of rolling on the shoulder as done with the Shoulder Roll the arm is left extended to avoid body contact with the snow. There are several possibilities but it starts with the basic Shoulder Roll.

Technique

1 Stand across the hill with the downhill pole planted behind the body. From here you must aim your body to contact the snow on the back of the uphill shoulder.

2 Gently jump off both skis and drive the uphill hand and arm between the downhill ski pole and the body. This will create the necessary rotation to twist the body.

3 Brace the impact by rolling off the hand, waist, arm, shoulder and neck.

4 As you are rolling, the skis must be twisted so that they land together, facing the proper direction.

5 The momentum will carry you on to your skis, and then stand up.

Helpful Hints

• You must go for it. Wait for a powder day or when the snow is soft.
Once an attempt is made the trick becomes easier.
• Twist the legs sideways while rolling so that the skis don't end up stuck in the snow.

Using your poles

Some top ballet competitors such as Peter Lindecke and Stephanie Sloan don't use poles while performing their routines. They feel they restrict the hand movement and the fluidity of the routine. Many other competitors, like Mark Stiegemeier, use their poles to add character to their runs. One competitor, at the end of his run, throws a pole into the air, spinning it three times and catching it right on the grip. Another possibility is to hold the poles as if they were a violin. This looks especially good with an Outrigger. Tucking them under the arms also adds variation to any trick and looks especially good with spins. They can be used for much more than just balance, though when learning new tricks that is what they are most suited for. It is up to the individual to find other things that can be done with poles. There are some tricks where they are required because weight is placed on them. There are two different styles of gripping the poles. One is the normal grip, where the ski pole is at right angles to the arm. The other, used most often with pole tricks, is gripping the top of the handle so that the pole and arm form a straight line. This position allows more height when standing up on the poles. Hands should not be placed in the straps when executing pole tricks. Many competitors take the straps off altogether. With straps there is a chance of falling on the poles, pulling an arm or finger or even stabbing yourself. Without straps the poles can be quickly disposed of so that they won't do any of these things.

TIP STAND

A Tip Stand involves standing on the ski tips, placing the ski poles in front for balance. There are several ways to reach this position. The easiest is to find a flat area that is hard enough to stop the tips from sinking when stood upon. Stand in a normal ski position, placing the poles forward. Place one ski behind you so that the tip is in the snow near where the tail of the other ski lies. The back of the upright ski should touch your back. Move slowly backwards so that the weight is felt on that ski and it feels like you are sitting on your boot. As you balance your weight on this tip and the two poles bring the other ski to a position where the tip is about one foot away and parallel to the other. From here it is just a matter of adjusting the ski and poles until you are comfortable. Once this is done try jumping up to a tip stand.

Technique

1 Rock arms, shoulders and body straight backwards. Keep the skis apart for more balance.

2 Lunge forward on to the poles that have been placed about three feet in front of the tips.

3 The body must come forward so that the tips will stop in the snow.

4 As the body comes forward the knees are bent so that the body doesn't keep going right over the poles.

5 Rock back on to the skis and boots so that the pressure is relieved from the poles. Find the most comfortable position and then try to stand there without the poles.

Helpful Hints

● The body must lunge forward, not upwards. Only then will the tips stay in the snow. If you lunge forward and end up on your front you have made the proper move. Now try to catch yourself with the poles.

● To reduce the amount of force necessary when jumping on to the tips find a gently descending slope and ski slowly down the fall line into the trick. When the proper technique is used, skiing into the Tip Stand requires almost no effort.

● To come down, pivot the legs sideways and let the skis land on their edges. Falling straight backwards could result in a broken tip if it has sunk into the snow. Another alternative is to push the poles away, fall on to the hands and do a front roll.

DAFFY STAND

A Daffy Stand gets its name from the same position used in the aerial event. A Daffy is when one leg is forward and the other backward. To get into this position follow the steps for a Tip Stand until the moment when the second ski is brought behind. At this point, instead of going backwards, place the ski in front with the bottom end in the snow.

A variation of this is the Tail Stand where weight is distributed between the tails of both skis and the poles. These tricks are great to practise during bad weather and long lift lines. Just make sure, when practising, that no one is standing too close.

TIP ROLL

This is a difficult trick to attempt. It is best to learn the Tip Roll in stages. At first, follow the directions without skis. Then practise with only the uphill ski. Doing these preliminary exercises before attempting the final form will give an understanding of the motions involved and will enable anyone to succeed.

Technique

1 Stand on the slope with skis at a right angle to the fall line. Place the poles about two feet directly below the boots. Hold the poles with the hands over the top of the grips. Bend the legs and prepare to jump.

2 The jump must be made so that the body is projected straight down the fall line over the poles. At the same time, the head is lifted and held high. This will add more height and time to the trick. With the weight on the poles the legs can be brought up behind the body and pivoted.

3 The legs are pivoted around the poles 360 degrees so the skier lands facing the same direction as before only below the poles.

Helpful Hints

• It takes a lot of effort to jump over the poles the first time with skis on. Build up confidence by practising with one ski or no skis.

• If the tips won't stay in the snow it is because the legs are not being bent and/or not enough weight is on the poles.

• Short skis are a big help with the Tip Roll.

• Once the mechanics are understood a Tip Roll becomes easier by skiing into it. With a bit of speed and a good edge set momentum will do the work that the legs had to do whilst in a stationary position.

WINDMILL

There are many variations of the Tip Roll. Most of them need the extra height and time provided by being skied into. Before any of the more difficult pole tricks are tried the basic Tip Roll should be well understood. It teaches the initiation step that is used in all tip roll tricks. The variations occur once in the air as demonstrated with the Windmill. This trick is a Tip Roll with an added twist at the end.

Technique

1 Ski across the hill and prepare for the pole plant.

2 Give a strong edge set and place the poles as described in the Tip Roll. Bend the knees to initiate the spring.

3 The weight is over the poles and the legs pivot around them as in the basic Tip Roll.

4 The momentum brought about by the speed of skiing into the trick, and the edge, will carry the body down the hill. The tips are lifted off the snow and the body and skis are twisted so that they "Windmill" around.

5 A landing is made by facing the opposite direction as when started. The body has rotated 540 degrees. With another half twist and landing backwards a 720 degree Tip Roll would have been made.

Helpful Hints

• The quick spin is made at the top of the Tip Roll by pushing off the poles with the hands and rotating the feet.

• When this trick becomes easy try landing in an Outrigger.

TIP ROLL INTO SHEA GUY

Technique

1 From the peak of a normal Tip Roll, as the lower ski is coming towards the snow, the uphill one should be held up in the air.

2 It will be brought over and twisted 180 degrees as the other lands on the snow.

3 Once both skis have contacted the snow the weight is transferred to the outside ski and a Shea Guy position is assumed.

Helpful Hints

● Think about doing a normal Tip Roll, landing on the inside ski and twisting the outside one 180 degrees.

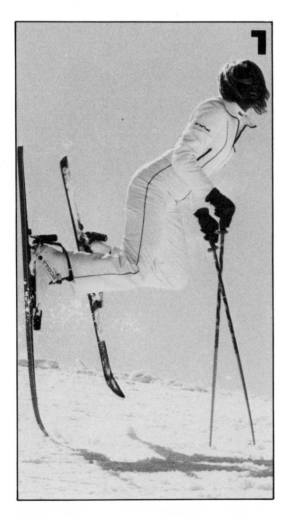

This trick involves crossing the skis after having started the Tip Roll. But one could also start with the skis crossed and then uncross them, or even keep them crossed throughout the trick. They are all difficult and require excellent timing.

Technique

1 Once at the top of the Tip Roll it is important to keep the weight well on top of the poles. By doing this properly, more time is allowed in the air to execute the crossover.

2 As the uphill ski is being lifted in the air the downhill one is being twisted underneath. It will become the surface ski. Weight is still maintained on the poles.

3 The landing is made in a crossover position. A Crossover 360 would be a good trick to follow with after landing.

Helpful Hints

• It takes time in the air to cross the skis over and still end up heading in the proper direction.

• The Tip Roll Crossover should end up the same way as the Windmill, which means rotating 540 degrees.

WONG BANGER

Many gymnastic moves are incorporated in ballet. They add excitement as well as variety to a routine. Wayne Wong was the first to bring such tricks to the ballet arena with a front pole flip which was named the Wong Banger. Wong because of his name and Banger because of what happens when the flip is done properly. Since then, many other gymnastic moves such as the Walk Over, Daigle Banger, Back Pole Somersaults and Hand Stands are common sights at competitions.

Technique

1 The Wong Banger should be learned without skis first. Have a spotter present so that he can help you flip all the way around or catch an unsuccessful attempt.

The key to success is kipping, or in other words, the motion of kicking the legs forward and underneath the body so that the feet land first. When the movements are understood find an area with soft snow and build a small wall of snow five inches high. Ski slowly straight down the fall line, aiming for the small mound. When the ski hits the mound jump forward, bracing the body with the poles. Kip to land back on the feet.

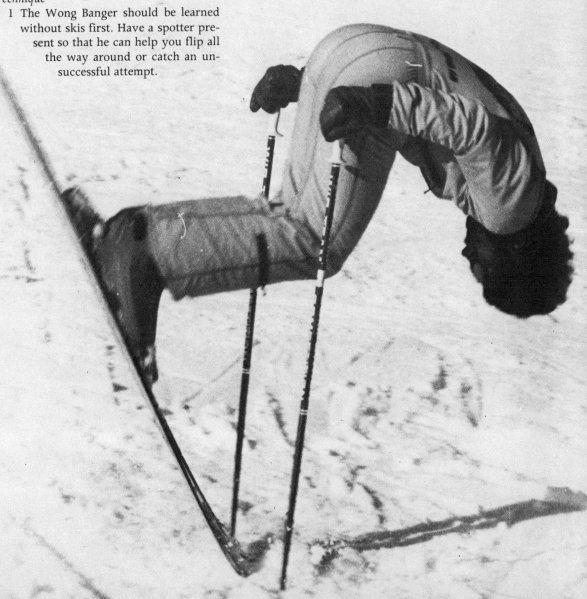

advanced ballet

REVERSE TIP DRAG 360

A lot harder than it looks. The Reverse Tip Drag 360 takes a special sense of balance and timing, especially during the start of the spin. Once initiated the spinning technique is the same as with the basic 360 spins.

Technique

1 Head straight down a gently inclining slope in a Reverse Crossover position. This position can be reached by either doing a Reverse Crossover (bringing around one ski behind the other) or from a Crossover position, placing the upper ski on the snow so that the surface ski is trailing behind. No matter how the position is arrived at it is dangerous because of the difficulty of un-crossing the legs quickly during a fall.

2 To initiate the spin let the tip of the ski that is left behind dig into the snow by applying pressure with the foot and leaning in its direction. This also makes the surface ski flat on the snow.

3 By keeping that ski flat and maintaining forward pressure the momentum from the initial Tip Drag will carry the spin 360 degrees.

4 The 360 is finished. Another 360 could be made by dragging the tip again or another trick can follow.

Helpful Hints
- Know the fundamentals of a One Ski 360 before trying this one.
- Lift the raised ski by twisting the ankle so that it stays out of the snow. It could get caught, causing a fall.

TAIL DRAG 360

The Tail Drag 360 is a graceful and flowing, spinning manoeuvre often seen in competition. Once the One Ski 360 has been well learned, the Tail Drag 360 will not cause any problem that a little practice won't take care of.

Technique

1 Traverse the slope and, as in all 360 spins, anticipate the initiation by counter rotating the upper body.

2 The momentum is started as the hands and body twist around. The weight stays on the uphill ski as the inside ski is lifted up.

3 The surface ski slides around the other ski in the snow.

4 As the sliding ski goes past the fall line the other ski comes down on the snow. The head is now turned in the direction to be skied.

When the lifted ski arrives on the snow, the weight is transferred to it.

The skis are brought parallel with the weight remaining on the inside ski in preparation for the next trick.

Helpful Hints
● The longer the ski can be held up in a horizontal position the better the trick looks.
● To avoid being stuck half way in the spin use more upper body rotation in the beginning.
● When the horizontal ski lands on the snow turn the body and head so that the weight is quickly transferred.

Technique

1 Ski across the hill and lift the uphill ski while guiding the traverse with the downhill ski.

2 Bring the uphill ski behind the body, keeping the weight forward on the surface ski.

3 Place the lifted ski behind you in a Shea Guy position.

4 Lean downhill so that the weight is transferred to the new downhill ski. Anticipate the new direction by turning the head.

5 With all the weight on the downhill ski lift the heel of the boot and pivot so that it ends crossed over the surface ski.

Keeping the surface ski flat on the snow will ensure the trick's completion by allowing it to spin another 180 degrees. Once in Crossover position it is possible to follow with more tricks.

Helpful Hints

● When swinging the uphill ski below the other, bring it parallel to the other. This is a hard position to hold so lift the other ski quickly so as to end up in the Crossover position.

● Once in a Shea Guy lift the uphill ski only a couple of inches off the snow and let the ski slide into proper position. Don't pick the ski up and try to force it. Make the transition as smoothly as possible.

3

4

5

WHISTLE

This trick gets its funny name from the fact that one of the skis spins so fast it starts to whistle; that is if one can get it going that fast. The Whistle is used by many freestylers including John Eveas, North American Overall Champion, and Alan Schonberger, three times North American Ballet Champion. It is a beautiful trick that is not difficult to learn.

Technique

1 With the downhill ski crossed over the other traverse a smooth slope at a moderate speed. Transfer the weight on to the crossed over ski or now uphill ski.

2 Pick up the downhill ski and start to pivot the surface ski as done in the Cross Twist. At the same time the other ski is pivoted 360 degrees in the same direction, only in the air. Keep this leg as straight as possible.

3 When the ski has almost come all the way around let the tail drag in the snow so that the rest of the ski can contact the snow more smoothly. If this is not done a jump is usually required to make contact with the snow, making the transition look rough.

4 The ski has spun 360 degrees and is headed in the same direction as in the beginning. The weight has been transferred to it.

5 The other ski is brought around so as to end up in the basic ballet stance.

Learning a Tip Roll and the method of keeping the tips in the snow has to be practised first with the poles. Even then the timing has to be spot on when doing a Tip Roll Without Poles because there is little room for error. The following sequence demonstrates the Tip Roll done down the hill but it can be done just as easily up the hill.

Technique

1 Prepare for the manoeuvre by aiming the arms down the hill and ski slowly across the hill. The body is held erect.

2 With a sweeping down motion of the hands and a bending of the knees the initiation of the jump is made.

3 As the hands come up the body jumps slightly forward and the tails of the skis are lifted behind and pivoted 180 degrees. The knees must do the work here. Only by bending and then turning will the skis come all the way around.

4 The trick ends skiing backwards.

Helpful Hints

• If the tips are not sticking in the snow it is probably because the knees are not bending enough.

• If problems persist practise more Tip Rolls with the poles.

CROSSOVER TIP ROLL WITHOUT POLES

As the name implies, this is a Tip Roll in the crossed over position without poles. It is more difficult than a simple Tip Roll due to the greater possibility of catching an edge while the skis are crossed over, otherwise the movements are the same. As there are many variations of Tip Rolls with poles, so there are with tricks that extend from Tip Rolls without poles. This is just one of them.

Technique

1 Lift one ski over the other while slowly skiing down the fall line. This can also be done from a traverse position.

2 Ski in a Crossover position with ski tips close together.

3 Hands and body come down as knees bend anticipating the initiation of the jump.

4 The body extends and, as in the Tip Roll, the knees bring the skis around 180 degrees.

5 The weight lands on the downhill ski.

6 Immediately after, the uphill ski is twisted 180 degrees over the surface ski as the head and shoulders twist around with it.

7 The weight is now on this ski and the other is brought in to join it.

Helpful Hints

● This trick should not be attempted until a simple Tip Roll is well executed. A secure landing has to be made in order to jump out of the Crossover position because balance is all on one ski.

● Jump out of the Crossover position as quickly as possible.

Otherwise known as an aerial 360, the Helicopter is the base for many of the advanced ballet tricks. Only so much can be done while keeping the skis on the snow, then it is time to get in the air. Learning the aerial 360 will open up a new world of tricks, many that are shown on the following pages. Before attempting a Helicopter with skis, practise turning 360 degrees in the air without any ski gear on. Get a feeling of what is happening. The more gymnastic experience one has the better and the easier it will be.

Technique

1 Choose a good mogul on an uncrowded slope. The mogul should be fairly pointed with a smooth area leading to it and soft snow on the landing side. If you spin to the left your left side should be facing uphill. Ski across the hill towards the bump of your choice and prepare to spin. This is done by bending low in the knees and counter rotating the upper body.

2 Keep your eye on the peak of the mogul. Just before the boots reach that summit is the time to pop, in other words, extend the legs and stretch the whole body to get as much height as possible. At this point rotation is started by the upper body rotating in the direction of the spin.

3 The feet are kept together and the body straight to get maximum spin.

4 Absorb the landing by bending the knees.

3

4

Helpful Hints
• When a Helicopter is done off a mogul a lot of rotation must be initiated off the snow because there is little time in the air.
• A good pop is more important than speed because more air time is had by going higher rather than longer. It also makes the body straight.
• For more explanations on Helicopters read the aerial section.

ONE LEG HELICOPTER

The procedure of turning 360 degrees in the air on one ski is the same as with two except more upper body rotation is needed to compensate for the power lost by only jumping off one leg. This trick can be done slowly and gracefully or can be made spectacular by adding lots of speed and distance. The One Leg Helicopter can also be done as an aerial stunt. It is then called a Royal Helicopter. As with the Helicopter initiate the spin off a mogul that has a definite peak. Use the bump to add time and distance. The more you master the trick the less a bump you need to get the skis into the air.

Technique

1 Ski across the hill at a fairly good speed. The upper body is facing slightly downhill with the weight on the downhill ski and the downhill arm also held back.

2 The spin is now being initiated and several movements will be needed to successfully complete the trick. The weight is transferred to the uphill ski and that leg is bent in preparation for the pop. The downhill ski is left behind as the upper body is rotating up the hill. The outside arm leads the body giving it the necessary rotating force to complete the 360 degree spin.

3 The jumping leg is fully extended and the body has been pushed straight up in the air. The head is leading the body around and looking for the landing. If the initial rotation was too weak the body would not spin the full 360 degrees. When this happens the ankle of the turning ski can be twisted to reach the desired direction.

4 Once the body and turning ski have reached 360 degrees the other ski returns to the snow.

Helpful Hints

● To initiate the spin, the body must be counter rotated as in the basic 360 Spin on One Ski. Only then can enough power be given to spin 360 degrees in the air.

● A good bump (mogul) will help when learning a One Leg Helicopter because not so much pop is needed to get the necessary air time and more concentration can be placed on the rotation.

● When the body is not extended straight in the air and the twist is not made around a straight axis the body will spin crookedly and the landing will be side on. If this problem exists practise the Helicopter.

HELICOPTER SPLIT

This trick is a slight variation on the One Leg Helicopter. The initiation steps and the spin are the same, only the landing is different.

Technique

1–2 Follow the procedure for the take off as in the One Leg Helicopter, a good pop off the uphill ski and good rotation with the upper body. This time though, keep the ski that is in the air well twisted behind the body.

3 Upon landing, instead of bringing the skis parallel let the tip of the twisted ski catch in the snow so that a Shea Guy position is reached. The skis are now split.

Helpful Hints
● Balance is much more precise for this trick. A firm landing must be made because the weight remains on one ski instead of quickly coming on to two skis as in the One Leg Helicopter. If balance is lost a quick recovery is very difficult.
● Balance must be maintained and the body rotation quickly stopped so that by bending the knee down the hill and catching the ski tip the ski will remain in the split position.

2

3

Two other variations of the Helicopter are done while one ski is crossed over the other. In the first both skis are flat on the snow, the downhill ski crossed over the uphill one. They remain in that position throughout the trick. The second variation, which is demonstrated here, is not quite as difficult but is equally dangerous due to the risk of falling while in a crossed leg position. Here the crossed over ski is not placed flat on the snow but held over the surface ski as in the Crossover 360. The technique is the same as with an Aerial 360, only be careful in the Crossover position.

Technique

1 Cross the uphill ski over the downhill ski so that the tip is on the uphill side. Always learn an Aerial 360 by starting the rotation up the hill.

2 Proceed into the trick with the body counter rotated and legs bent in preparation for the pop and spin.

3 The hands have come above the head to give additional height while at the same time twisting the shoulders and upper body to give the necessary rotation. Note that the leg of the surface ski is straight. This signifies that a proper pop has been made. Only when good height has been attained are these aerial 360s possible. The pop must be made straight up or the body will spin sideways.

4 When all is properly executed a balanced landing will be made with the legs absorbing the shock. The poles are ready to catch any small loss of balance.

Helpful Hints

● To gain confidence with this trick try rotating only half way. It is possible because of the crossed over position. Follow the procedure as described only don't rotate as hard. Turn 180 degrees in the air and the rest on the snow. As confidence increases, spend more time in the air until the entire 360 degrees is achieved.

● When landing the tip of the top ski can be used for balance but be careful. This is also the movement that is used to initiate a Crossover 360.

The Whoya is an aerial form of the Tip Drag 360. This demonstrates how a simple trick can become the basis for one more demanding and spectacular. In this case, an extension of the legs and rotation in the air add new dimensions to a basic ballet trick. It is also much more difficult. Lots of practice is needed to feel comfortable while rotating in the air.

Technique

1 While skiing across the hill the tip of the uphill ski is placed in the snow so that the two skis are at right angles to each other. Both skis are kept close to the snow.

2 By applying pressure to that tip and making the other ski flat the skis will turn as described in the Tip Drag 360. To do the Whoya the legs must be bent and the body counter rotated to prepare for the initiation of the aerial rotation.

3 An extension is made off the surface ski while the other ski remains at a right angle to it. The hands and body have been twisted in the direction of the rotation. The hands are lifted high to give more height. Note the straightness of the extended leg.

4 The landing is made on the same ski as is used when taking off. The other ski has remained at ninety degrees during the rotation.

5 A secure landing enables continued movement into a Shea Guy position.

Helpful Hints

• Don't start the pop too soon. Ski into the hill and use the compression acquired in the turn to set up the pop.

• It takes a lot of concentration to keep the tip dragged ski behind during the aerial rotation. If you don't succeed at first keep trying until you have a comfortable feeling for the rotation. As this part becomes understood it will be easier to concentrate on the rest.

AERIAL LEG BREAKER

1

2

To better understand the movements of an Aerial Leg Breaker go back to the description of a Leg Breaker with 180 degree Pivot. The skis go to the same places, only this time they twist through the air instead of sliding. This is a difficult trick because the legs are apart while in the air, which tends to slow down the rotation. But it is a dynamic trick because so much is happening. Unless one is familiar with this stunt it would be very difficult to understand how the skis end up crossed over each other.

Technique

1 As in all the rotational aerials the pop or extension is most important. The upper body has been counter rotated so that it is facing down the hill. It is now in the process of rotating over the uphill leg, which is bent in anticipation of the pop. The downhill ski is starting to drift backwards.

2 As the pop is made, the downhill ski is lifted so that the ski on the extended leg can pass underneath.

3 The rotational momentum increases as the legs come together in a Crossover position.

4 While in the air the surface ski changes. The ski that gave the pop will end up crossed over the downhill ski and the downhill ski will become the surface ski. By using the tip of the crossed over ski balance can be added on landing.

Helpful Hints

● A very strong exertion must be made to get maximum height. The rotation is slow because of the movements with the legs.

● Use a bump as described with the Helicopter for more air. Don't use speed. Try to jump high, not far. This also makes for a straighter axis.

This trick gets its name from the fact that when done properly the skis make a loud thump on landing. The Thumper is a complicated trick and difficult to perform. There is no half way point, or stage, that can be learned first. The whole movement must be done as one. The difficulty lies in gaining enough momentum to rotate more than 360 degrees while crossing one ski over the other. In a Helicopter the skis remain together so that the rotation is not slowed down. In a Thumper the skis come wide apart. This slows down the rotation as well as sending it off balance.

Technique

1 There are two motions that must be prepared for before the initiation of the trick. The first is a forward motion which is acquired by skiing down the hill fairly fast. The second is the rotational motion that is set up by counter rotating the upper body.

2 From here a turn is started on the outside ski while the inside ski and the body start their rotation.

3 An edge set from the outside ski and an extension of the leg provide the pop needed to get the trick into the air. At the same time the body and inside ski continue to rotate.

4 If the pop, rotation and speed going into the trick are enough then the skis will come around 360 degrees, but there is still another movement required. While the 360 is taking place the ski that gave the edge set must pass over the other ski.

5 It is on this ski (the same one used to initiate the trick), that the landing is made. The other ski ends up crossed over behind the ski landed on.

6 After a smooth landing the skier heads across the hill.

Helpful Hints

● During the initiation of the trick the inside ski must be brought well behind the body or the surface ski will not have room to pass over it.

● During the pop the body must be projected forward to keep the speed flowing to allow more air time.

● Some ballet skiers will use their poles to help initiate the spin. Some smoothness is lost but at least the trick is completed.

AXEL

New tricks have been brought about by freestylers looking for a chance to bring something new and different to their routines. Most ideas have been extensions of older tricks already performed on the snow while others have stemmed from outside the ski realm. The Axel is a figure skating manoeuvre that has been adapted to the bulkiness of skis. Whether on ice or snow, co-ordination and proper timing are needed to perform this trick correctly.

1

Technique
1 In preparation for the initiation of the pop and spin, the body is aimed down the hill and the knees are bent.

2 As the pop is made off the uphill ski the hands come over the head to provide additional height. While in the air the skis come together to speed up the rotation.

3 Once the 360 is complete the legs come apart to slow down the rotation and the landing is made on the opposite foot than was used to initiate the manoeuvre.

2

Helpful Hints
• Use a mogul when learning the Axel to give more height.
• Use the hands to add more height by having them lead the rotation and pop.
• This is a beautiful trick but takes a while to master. Don't be discouraged if a landing can't be made on the downhill ski. A bit of practice will take care of that.

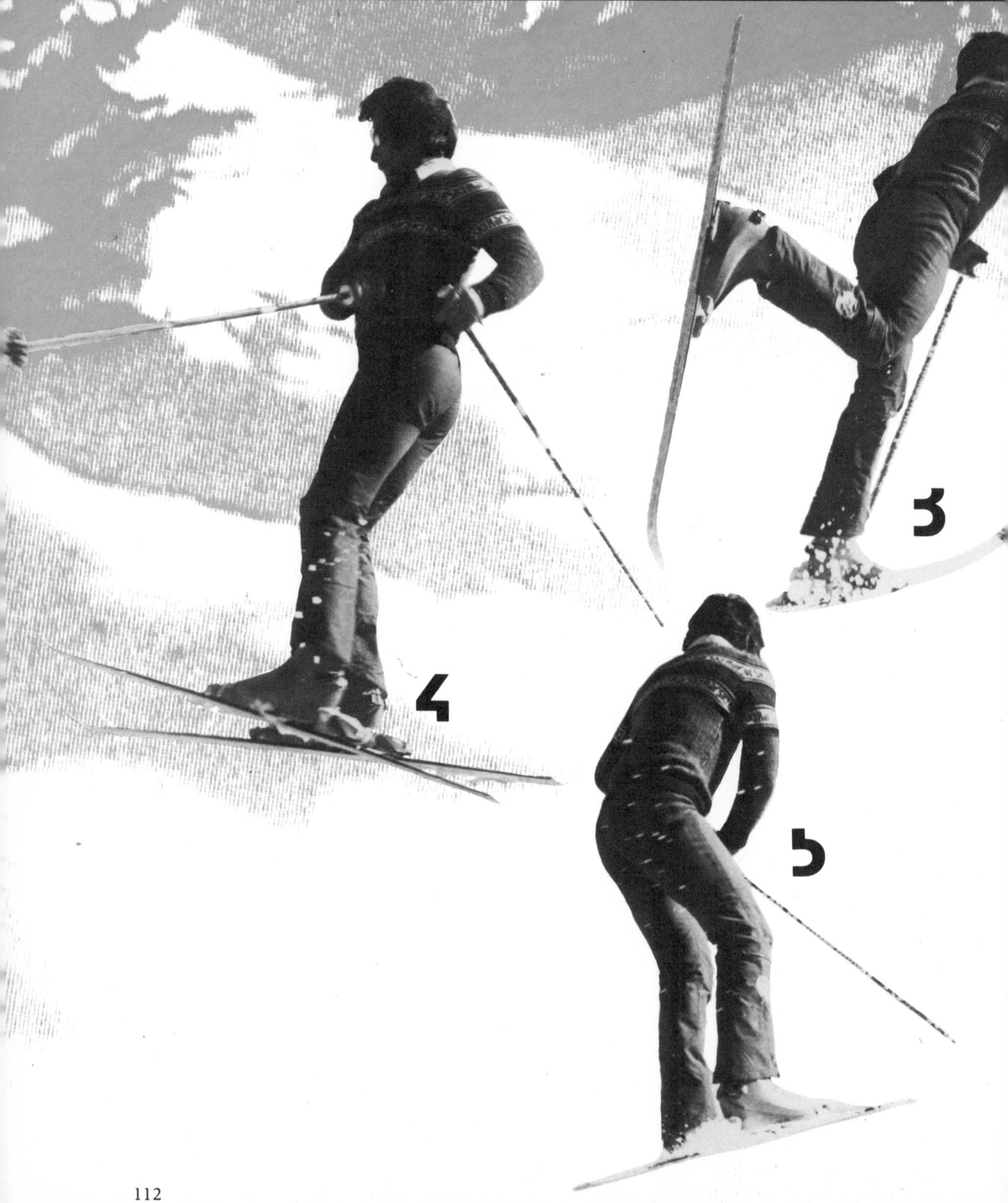
3
4
5

Rotating in the air one and a half times, twice, or off a flat, well prepared ballet slope takes a lot of practice and a complete understanding of the Aerial 360 manoeuvres. It also takes a desire to "go for it". Greg Athens, combined winner of the 1976 Chevrolet Freestyle Circuit, amazed everyone with his double Helicopters during his ballet run. The single spins teach the importance of a good extension or pop, plus the necessity of synchronising the initiation of the rotation. The proper form in the air must also be maintained or the manoeuvre will come to a shaky end. Because of the greater rotation when performing a $1\frac{1}{2}$ or double the precision and timing are critical, but if the single rotational tricks are mastered the $1\frac{1}{2}$ Axel will just be another step on the progression ladder.

Technique

1 Traverse the slope fairly fast with the downhill ski crossed over the other.

2 Put pressure on to the now uphill ski, bending the knee in preparation for the pop. The upper body is starting up the hill in the direction of the spin.

3 As the upper body passes over the uphill ski the leg extends and the trick is started. At the same instant the other ski is lifted up to let the extended ski pass underneath.

4 The legs and hands are held tightly to the body so that the rotation is increased.

5 A landing is made facing backwards, completing the one and a half spin.

Helpful Hints

● The $1\frac{1}{2}$ Axel can be practised by following these steps but only spinning once. As confidence builds so can the amount of rotation increase.

● Once the pop is made rotational speed can be gained by wrapping the arms quickly and tightly around the body.

● It is more difficult landing backwards than forwards, so a good axis must be kept during the rotation. This is done by jumping high and keeping the body straight while rotating.

AERIAL ACROBATICS

Go For it

Jumping, otherwise known as aerial acrobatics, was always the most spectacular and anticipated event of a freestyle competition. It had the excitement and tension of a car race. Spectators came to see who would win but also who would crash. They were seldom disappointed. Back in 1972 and 1973 big crashes were the order of the day as competitors tried just about anything to become number one. These skiers were the pioneers of Hot Dogging, pushing themselves to their physical limit, not knowing the rules or just how far they could go. It was the time when the shout "Go For It" rang in the ears of many young skiers who thought that if someone else could flip on skis so could they. These thrill seekers hoped that on the day of competition they could put it all together. Their belief was that with a bit of luck an upright landing would be made and first prize would be theirs.

But in the States during the winter of 1973 two freestylers weren't so lucky. Scott Maringo and Peter Hershorn were permanently paralysed from injuries received while attempting double back flips, one trying it for the first time in a competition.

It took the reality of these two accidents and the permanent injury they produced to open the eyes of competitors, sponsors and organisers to the dangers of landing on the snow upside down. It was a turning point for the aerial event as well as for freestyle in general. At Sun Valley, during the final freestyle competition of 1973, no inverted jumps were allowed. In 1974 strict rules governed all three disciplines, especially aerial acrobatics. Jumpers could no longer simply try anything they wanted to but had to qualify each inverted jump before a safety committee. The committee also controlled the jump and the landing hill to make sure they were as safe as possible as well as deciding whether or not a competition should be cancelled due to bad conditions. Judging also changed. Before the accidents points were given to those who were most daring, while afterwards judges were interested in the degree of perfection achieved. A simple jump would score higher if done perfectly than a more difficult one executed poorly.

Today the aerialists' motto is still "Go For It", only its yell has a much different meaning. It means go for perfection, do it right. An aerial event these days is more like a gymnastic tournament. The stage is set by snow cats with large ploughs to construct jumps to standardised dimensions. The landing hill is a specified length and a leveller is used to test its angle. The jumps themselves have a predetermined shape and are placed at a certain distance behind the landing hill. The competitors practise on jumps of the same dimensions as well as on trampolines, diving boards and artificial ski jumps. They train all summer as well as studying and discussing the technical aspects of aerial acrobatics. In 1973 competitors participated in all three events. Today the freestyle circuit is much more specialised, with many top competitors participating in only one event.

This total commitment to the sport has produced an incredible growth in the development of freestyle that is particularly evident in the aerial discipline. Before 1972 very few skiers had ever *thought* of doing a flip. But when the Americans began offering cars and big prize money as incentives many skiers were ready to try anything. Many jumps were attempted but few perfected. Several jumpers such as Ed Lincoln and Bob Theobold gave an insight into the future. The winter of 1974 provided an atmosphere which encouraged people to improve on what had been tried before. With the new safety regulations a competitor had to demonstrate full control of his jump before he could perform it in competition. Many good back and front flips were seen. A few aerialists perfected the moebius (a full somersault with a full twist). By 1975 a solid base had been established and competitors were ready to push forward with new confidence. Moebius flips, double helicopters, and long flips over 30 metres were the winning jumps.

In 1976 jumping fans were given a real treat. A group of gymnasts from Salt Lake City who had spent more time in the air than on skis, joined the PFA Freestyle tour. They brought with them a wealth of "air" knowledge that would advance the aerial event beyond belief. The final competition of the year demonstrated what had been learned. Double flips were common, Manfred Kastner achieved a triple back flip, and Ed Lincoln demonstrated what would happen next year—a double flip with a full twist.

During 1977 almost every combination of double and single flip, spin and twist was executed to perfection. The competitors weren't yet ready for triple flips so they wisely stayed away from them. But it wouldn't be too long before they too became just another jump.

During the past four years a deep understanding of aerial acrobatics has been gained by the intense efforts of many freestylers. The principles learnt are passed down to any skier who wants to get some air. Freestyle schools throughout the world have taught hundreds to perform daffys, backscratchers, helicopters, front tucks, back layouts, moebiuses and many other aerials. But most important is that they have been taught safely. No longer must an aspiring aerialist challenge fate by having to learn everything for himself. Instead, a safe progression can be followed with a qualified instructor explaining everything along the way. This advanced method of learning does not detract from the thrill of success. In order to perform a flip on skis one must always "Go For It". The excitement created when one succeeds for the first time is beyond comparison. This sensation is not limited to inverted jumps but is also experienced in the uprights. Particular emphasis has been placed on safety for competitive aerial acrobatics, instruction and practice. It has been discovered that air sense, the ability to know where your body is while in the air, can be acquired safely and quickly by practising rotational manoeuvres elsewhere other than on snow. Trampolines, diving boards, mini tramps, floor gymnastics and artificial ski ramps with landings of water, hay or an air bag have provided the means to do this. What used to take a couple of winter seasons to learn can now be achieved in a couple of months—without risk.

Aerial acrobatics is much more than just flipping. Every time a skier jumps off a mogul or a cornice he gets some air. Ski areas are full of natural jumps that are available to every level of skier. They offer an opportunity for fun and excitement that shouldn't be passed by. There are fundamental points and safety tips which are explained in the Upright Aerial section and which will be useful to any skier. Jumping and learning a little "air sense" is a part of everyday skiing. Being able to add a couple of tricks makes it all the better. Any upright trick that is described in the following section can be done off a natural transition on the mountain. One doesn't have to get involved with gymnastics and the techniques of inverted aerials to enjoy the thrill of "getting air". It is all relative. Everyone has their own limit whether it be a triple flip or a spread eagle off a small mogul. No matter what your skiing ability or past jumping record, extend yourself just a bit, add a little excitement to your skiing and "Go For It".

The aerial stage

A proper aerial stage provides the best and safest conditions under which to learn different aerial manoeuvres, as well as for acquiring a sense for the air. Because of its form the skier is sent gently into the air and lands on the snow at the most comfortable angle, reducing most of the shock while getting maximum distance. The jumper follows the same path every time he jumps so that there are no surprises. This enables him to concentrate completely on the manoeuvre he is performing. All jumps vary within certain degrees. During competitions and professional freestyle classes the dimensions are kept as close to the norm as possible. A lot of work goes into the construction and maintenance of a jump. It must be constantly watched to control which skiers go off, and it takes up a lot of area on the hill. For these reasons, plus the skiers' own safety, it is best to join a freestyle class where the jump is built correctly and someone else is taking care of it.

The aerial stage consists of many different parts —they will differ slightly, depending on how advanced the jumper is—but they should always be in perfect condition to allow full concentration on the actual manoeuvre.

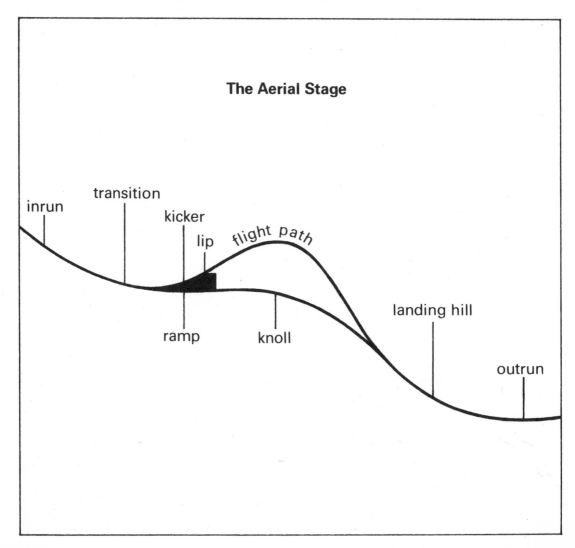

The Aerial Stage

inrun

transition

kicker

lip

flight path

ramp

knoll

landing hill

outrun

THE INRUN This is the part of the slope that precedes the jumping ramp. It should not be very steep but always running downhill. It should be perfectly smooth with no bumps that might affect the straight running of the skis. It should be wide enough so that if the aerialist decides not to jump there is room to ski off to the side. A jumper should walk up the inrun until he reaches a spot from which he can ski straight down without breaking and reach the ramp at the desired speed. If an inrun is too steep it will be too difficult to control the speed entering the jump. It also makes for a very quick run, in that it doesn't allow enough time to prepare for the jump. If an inrun is too flat the skis will tend to slow down as the jump approaches, especially if the snow is wet and soft. It is difficult to regulate the speed when the inrun is too steep or too flat. This will create another factor to think about while skiing into the jump and it will detract from the concentration that must be placed on the manoeuvre itself.

TRANSITION The point where the downhill becomes the uphill is called the transition area. A proper transition is a long gradual change that is not felt by the skier as it is passed over. When an inrun is too steep an abrupt change must take place to go up off the jump. This is a bad transition that will tend to throw the body backwards just at the moment when it is time to prepare for the manoeuvre. In order to compensate for this the knees must absorb the transition as though it were a hole in the snow. This detracts from the concentration that should be exclusively on the manoeuvre.

KNOLL The spot where the hill starts sloping downward and from where a safe landing can be made is called the knoll. This is the start of the landing hill. A jumper must pass over this point before landing otherwise he will land on the flat, which can give a strong jolt to the legs and body. This is controlled by always having enough speed down the inrun. The advantage of having an instructor present is that he knows how much speed is needed to pass over the knoll without landing at the bottom of the jump.

LANDING HILL The landing hill should be long enough to provide a good slope for the type of jumpers using it but not so long that too much speed is gained before getting to the outrun. It should have an even slope of about 35 degrees from top to bottom. If the landing hill is too steep the jumper free falls from too high up, which can be dangerous. If it is too flat then the landing will be very hard, causing hard shocks on the knees as well as the head. Falling on such a surface can be dangerous too. A landing hill should be made up of firmly packed, fresh snow. If it is too soft the skis will dig deep into the snow on landing which might lead to a fall. When the snow is too hard it is foolish to jump because of the danger from a possible fall. When hard conditions exist a snow cat or snow picks and shovels should be used to loosen up the snow. As jumpers land on the landing hill holes are formed where their skis first contact the snow. These must constantly be filled up and smoothed out so that the following jumpers don't jump into a big rut. Holes created by jumpers who have fallen must be treated in the same way.

OUTRUN A large area for the skiers to slow down after jumping is very important. Usually a jumper is in control when he lands and can stop straight away but there is always the chance of a bad landing and a struggle for recovery. If the outrun is too steep, or full of bumps and soft snow, a recovery becomes very difficult and the possibility of injury is high, due to the speed that has been accumulated from the top of the inrun. A gentle transition is also needed between the landing hill and the outrun for the same reason; as between the inrun and the jump. The outrun should always be clear of any obstacles or spectators.

THE RAMP No matter how much an attempt is made at standardising the jumping ramps there will always be a difference of opinion on how curved the kickers should be, and how close to the knoll the jump should be placed. Aerialists get used to their own dimensions and even though the differences are small, when one must make that slight adjustment, it is another consideration to be thought of while jumping. Depending on the capabilities of the aerialist the ramp will be placed either close to, or far back, from the knoll. To provide for the safest jumping the highest point of the flight path should pass directly over the knoll. This means that half the jump is completed before passing over the downhill slope which, in turn, ensures the smoothest possible landing because one slides down the landing hill instead of hitting straight on it. It is the same principle that enables Nordic jumpers to fly so far and not be jolted out of their boots upon landing. This means that the further one jumps, whether an upright jump or a flip is executed, the further back the ramp should be placed. When a jumper is getting started he won't jump too far so the ramp should be closer. The aerial stage should be set so that most of the jumpers are landing near the middle of the landing hill. The distance between the transition and the knoll should be approximately 30 feet so that there is enough room to position the ramp to suit individual jumpers.

KICKERS The shape of the ramp changes according to the jumps to be performed. These different shapes are known as kickers and there are three types. A floater or upright kicker is a long and gently curved or straight platform used for upright jumps and helicopters. Its angle is set to give the skier distance without setting him off balance from too much of a transition. The floater is usually set further back from the knoll. A back kicker has more of an upward angle and consistent curve to initiate back flips. Its angle will send the jumper higher but not as far as the floater. This added height helps in making a smooth, even backwards rotation. The front kicker has more curve than either of the others. A skier will jump out, over the lip or top of the jump. The sharp angle of the kicker will help leave the skis behind as the body goes forward. Each kicker is designed to help with the initiation of its respective jump. A kicker must always be as smooth as possible and kept hard. If the snow is soft the skis will dig into it and change its shape. The kicker should always be checked to make sure its shape remains the same. The lip should always be a definite line across the top of the kicker. It is from this point that the jump is started. Missing the lip on the jump would be like a plane trying to take off on an aircraft carrier after it had passed over the end.

Jumping off a proper aerial stage is a great experience. Anybody who wants to try it can go further and higher than they ever thought possible. A little practice and any of the upright manoeuvres are quickly learned. Whether one learns from a professional freestyle instructor or manages to build his own jump, always keep safety as the top consideration. Several safety points to remember are:

1 Keep a fence around the aerial stage, especially the landing hill and outrun to keep skiers and spectators out of harm's way (theirs and yours).

2 Keep the kickers in good shape.

3 Have the jumps placed at the proper distance from the knoll.

4 Always make sure the landing area is clear before each jump.

5 Fill all holes on the landing hill before continuing.

6 Don't jump alone.

7 Don't attempt a new upright manoeuvre unless it is completely understood before going off the jump.

8 Never try a flip unless proper instruction is present and the movements have been learned elsewhere other than on snow.

9 Don't wear safety straps or pole straps when jumping, but do wear ski stoppers.

10 Go for perfect form before big air.

11 Don't jump when the landing is too hard.

12 Don't jump over the landing hill.

13 Decide on the manoeuvre to be performed before heading towards the jumping ramp.

14 When jumping is over for the day, leave the slope in good shape so that it is ready for the next time.

Different Types of Kickers

front

back

floater or upright

Upright aerials

Upright aerials can best be learned off a proper aerial stage, but there are still many naturally built places on any mountain, such as moguls, cornices and ridges where one can get some air and practise the aerial technique. This technique boils down to one basic principle—the pop. The pop is an upward extension of the legs and body just before the moment when the boots pass over the lip of the jump. This movement sets up every jump so that the body will pass properly through the air. Without the pop the body will not get enough height or be in the proper position to do acrobatic manoeuvres. The pop is used to initiate a jump while skiing through the moguls. Without a good pop aerial ballet manoeuvres are just about impossible. Any aerial manoeuvre, whether upright or inverted, will not have the proper height and flotation if the pop is left out.

This extension, or pop, can be practised without skis. Stand on a flat surface with knees well bent and arms held low. Jump straight into the air as high as possible, keeping the legs extended, the body straight and the arms in front. For an example of this position refer to the upright jump with pop (p.126). This position should be maintained while in the air. Upon landing, absorb the shock by bending the knees. This movement can be practised off small bumps on the hill. Instead of riding over the top of them pop and see how much height can be obtained. A little practice off small bumps on the slope will go a long way when it's time to go off a professional jump. Once a skier has learned the proper technique of the "pop" and has gained a feeling for the air (air sense) any upright manoeuvre is a short step away. The following progression of jumps will show the easiest way to master all the different upright

aerials. Though they can all be learned first on snow, practising the various positions on a trampoline or diving board first will speed up the learning process. It will also help to better understand the various manoeuvres.

When skiing off a large jump for the first time it is always best to proceed with caution and get a "feel" for the jump before trying any acrobatic manoeuvres. To get this feeling, ski down the inrun with just enough speed to clear the knoll and, instead of popping, keep the legs stiff without extending them. After this test, the speed of the inrun, the shape of the kicker, its angle of trajectory and the condition of the landing hill will all be well known. If something is wrong it can be fixed. If everything is in order then jumping can be started with confidence. For a skier who has never been off an acrobatic jump before, or has only made a few attempts, the first jump should be taken with a few more points in mind. Have someone, preferably a qualified freestyle instructor, tell you where to start from. One must have just enough speed to arrive on the top of the landing hill. Too much speed can cause a beginner to experience fear—that will make him tense and the subsequent loss of confidence is dangerous. Once headed down the inrun the skis should be about six inches apart, with knees bent and arms forward. Hold this position when going off the ramp. Don't absorb the jump but stiffen the legs so that the trajectory of the kicker is followed. A smooth flight will follow until the touchdown is made, where the legs are relaxed and bent to absorb the landing. A good outrun is crucial because most beginners are a little tense and need lots of room to slow down.

When learning to jump for the first time, or going off a new ramp, a good stance in the air as well as on the snow is a necessity. It will enable anybody to fly through the air and make a secure landing. The key to success is holding the same stance throughout the jump until the landing, when the legs must be bent to absorb the slight shock. Confidence is also needed. It can be gained through a qualified instructor, by observing others, or practising on smaller jumps. Of course a combination of the three is best. A Tip Drop, which is done by bending the knees so that the skis aim downward, has been added to this most basic jump to demonstrate a slight variation.

Technique

1 Find a spot on the inrun for your starting point. Assume the proper stance as soon as possible: skis about six inches apart and parallel, knees bent, upper body bent slightly forwards, arms apart and forward for balance, and head looking forward at the lip (peak of the jump). The legs are loose to maintain control over the skis on the inrun.

2 The same bent position is held while skiing over the transition area but now the legs must stiffen so as not to be absorbed by the kicker.

3 A slight extension has been made with the legs to compensate for the pressure exerted by the upward aim of the kicker but the legs are still bent. At the moment of passing over the lip the hands are brought gently forward to keep the body straight.

4 Position (3) can be maintained throughout the flight and a secure landing will follow. But often the take off is improperly made and the body doesn't remain upright. If the hands and body are not brought forward, or one sits back while skiing off the kicker, the body will fall backwards. If one jumps too far forward he might land on his head instead of his skis. If the body is not kept square and equal or pressure has not been kept on both skis as the skier leaves the ramp, he will go sideways. Even if these mistakes are made going off the ramp they can still be corrected in the air. When one is sitting back in the air a Tip Drop will bring the body forward. If the body is too far forward counter rotating with the arms will help to straighten things out. When going sideways the best thing to do is aim one leg at the ground and make a good recovery.

5 The same position (3) is returned to for the landing. Landing with legs bent allows the skier to absorb the shock.

Helpful Hints

● A well executed jump is determined by the take off. Minor corrections can be made in the air but then the jump is not neat. Just the right amount of forward motion must be started so that the skis are flat on landing.

● During one's first jump, it is important to start with a good stance and get used to the aerial stage. This usually comes after a few jumps. Once your confidence is up it is time to go to the next stage— the pop.

UPRIGHT JUMP WITH POP

The pop sets up body position in the air as well as adding additional height, length and flotation to the manoeuvre. In order to make any jump smooth a good extension off the lip is necessary. The following sequence shows how to initiate the pop and keep the body quiet in the air. Also the proper landing technique is shown. Once these basics become natural any upright manoeuvre is just an easy step away. But without "air sense" learned from this basic upright jump any attempt at an acrobatic position will be rushed and incomplete. Aquire "air sense" and also the feeling for a new jump by taking several straight upright jumps with a good pop.

Technique

1 Always try to ski straight into the ramp. Sometimes a snowplough to slow down or a bit of skating to speed up is needed, but after one go the proper speed should be known. Ski down the inrun in the same stance as described in the Tip Drop without Pop, keeping the eyes on the lip.

2 Instead of maintaining that position, the knees are going to bend low at the transition point so that they are prepared to extend at the right moment. The eyes are still on the lip.

3 The boots are right on the lip of the ramp. An extension, or pop, is being made at this point. This will give maximum height. If the pop is given too soon it is the same as making the ramp smaller. Only the bottom portion is used instead of the whole ramp. If the pop comes too late the legs are pushing against air and it will have the same effect as if no pop was given. Timing is important. While skiing down the inrun the eyes must focus on the lip so that the pop happens at exactly the right moment. This will guarantee a good flight so long as everything is in balance.

The extension is complete. The skis are headed up at the same angle as the kicker. Legs are straight, the hips are in and the arms are forward to balance the body if necessary.

4 The skis are now parallel with the horizon. The body is coming forward to follow the slope of the ground underneath. This is done during the pop. It is part of the "air sense" that is developed as one jumps. It is controlled by jumping slightly forward off the lip. Refer back to (3) and notice how the body is bent at the waist. This is enough to do the job. The hands have also been lifted forward to lead this subtle motion.

5 The skis are now parallel with the landing hill. They will land flat on the snow because the proper forward thrust was initiated off the lip. The body has not had to change its position. A balanced, secure jump has been made.

6 To land after such a jump the legs bend slightly to prepare for absorbing the shock of contacting the ground. Landing with stiff legs will give the whole body a jolt.

7 After contact with the snow the legs and body bend to absorb the shock.

Helpful Hints

● Make sure the aerial stage is in good shape especially the ramp and the shape of the kicker before jumping.

● Go off the ramp without a full pop first.

● Practise the pop on natural terrain before using it in an acrobatic jump.

● The main problem is usually a lack of confidence. An instructor is the best way to gain confidence. Once a little "air sense" is gained and one is not afraid of a kicker that points into space, jumping becomes much easier.

● A jump is always easier than it looks. Most skiers adapt quickly to jumping and after a couple of jumps have no problem working on better technique.

STAR

The Star has exactly the same movements as the Back Scratcher, except that the skis are spread apart at the tips leaving the tails together.

MULE KICK or SIDE KICK

The Mule Kick is an extreme example of action–counteraction. Two different movements must be executed, making this one of the hardest single upright aerials. Not only must the arms be pulled backwards to compensate for the skis underneath but, because the skis are also to the side, the shoulders and arms must be twisted in that direction too. The more the skis are to the side and the more the upper body is counter-rotated the better the Mule Kick position.

TWISTER

The Twister is a good manoeuvre for the bumps because the skis stay parallel with the terrain. The skis twist sideways while the upper body counteracts in the opposite direction. The legs should remain straight. If counteraction does not take place a rough side landing will result.

SPREAD EAGLE

This is the first aerial acrobatic manoeuvre to learn as it is the easiest. It is the easiest because the position does not unbalance the body while in the air. Once the pop has been made both legs are pushed to opposite sides as wide as possible. The arms usually go out to the sides or above the head. Beginners often wonder whether they will be able to get their legs back together before the landing. Freestyle is not that old but records have been kept, and to this day no one has ever landed in a spread eagle position. It seems that the body has a natural way of protecting itself and the legs will always come together in time. Spread Eagles are often done in the moguls because they can be done quickly and easily without loss of balance and the tips remain parallel to the slope so that there is no risk of catching a tip in the snow.

Technique

1 Follow the same steps as with the upright jump with pop—only once in the air spread the skis as wide apart as possible and hold that position until just before the landing. Bring the skis together and land.

Helpful Hints

● Most important with all acrobatic aerials is to perform the trick after the pop. Jump into the air first and then spread the skis apart. If this is not done the strength of the pop will be lost.

IRON CROSS

The basics are the same as a Back Scratcher. Ski tips down and crossed, make an Iron Cross. Be sure to uncross the iron before landing.

(For illustrations of the tricks on this page see the following colour section.)

Garth Valentine working out at Davas, Switzerland.

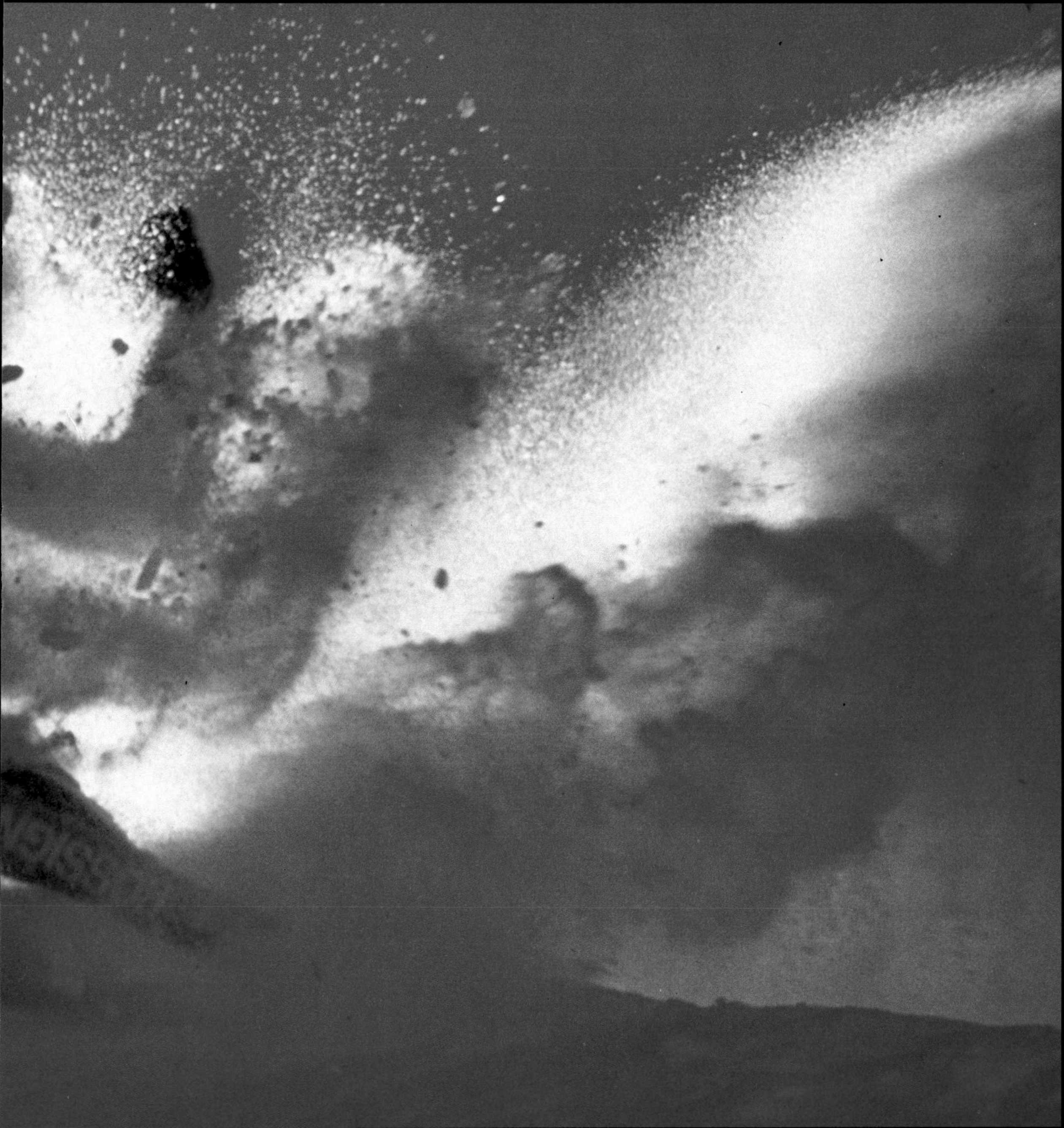

Spreadeagles.

In a class of its own the Zudnick is a direct **descendant of Nordic ski flying. The body is bent** forward with hand placed behind near the hips. When repeated several times in a row it is called a Wood Pecker.

BACK SCRATCHER

The Back Scratcher is a prime example of an action–counteraction upright aerial. The body has a set trajectory from the lip of the ramp to the landing hill as explained in the Upright Jump with Pop. If the initiation of the jump, or the pop, is not correct then the air time will be spent correcting the mistake made at the take off. The body should have a smooth flight from beginning to end so that the skis land flat without any correction necessary during the flight. Once this stability in the air is reached all upright aerials are possible. These aerials involve an action–counteraction—in other words when part of the body twists in any direction while in the air some other part must twist in the opposite direction to compensate for it. As in the Daffy, when one leg went forward and the other backwards the arms provided the counteraction by going in the opposite direction of the legs. The action–counteraction keeps the body's flight straight in the air and makes for a good landing.

Technique

1 The same secure inrun is made with body relaxed and concentration on the take off.

2 A good pop, with legs extended and hips in, is made to send the skier on the proper trajectory.

3 Once in the air the legs are pulled underneath the body so that the skis are pointing straight down and the tails are against the back. The arms and shoulders are pulled back to provide the counteraction to stop the body falling forward.

4 As the skis come off the back, the pressure is released from the arms and shoulders to slow down the counteraction.

5 The landing position is the same as with any aerial stunt. The skis land square on the snow and the legs absorb the shock.

Helpful Hints

● A full Back Scratcher should not be attempted straight away. Starting with a Tip Drop one can bring the skis further back while counteracting with the arms and shoulders until the full position is reached.

● This trick must be first tried on a professional jump. Practising this off a natural transition can be dangerous if a tip is caught in the snow.

● It is a good idea to practise this on a trampoline or diving board.

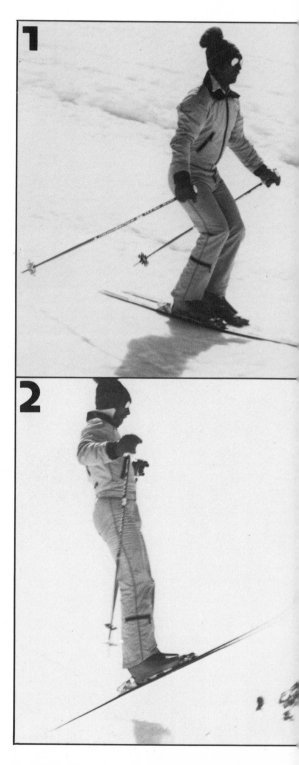

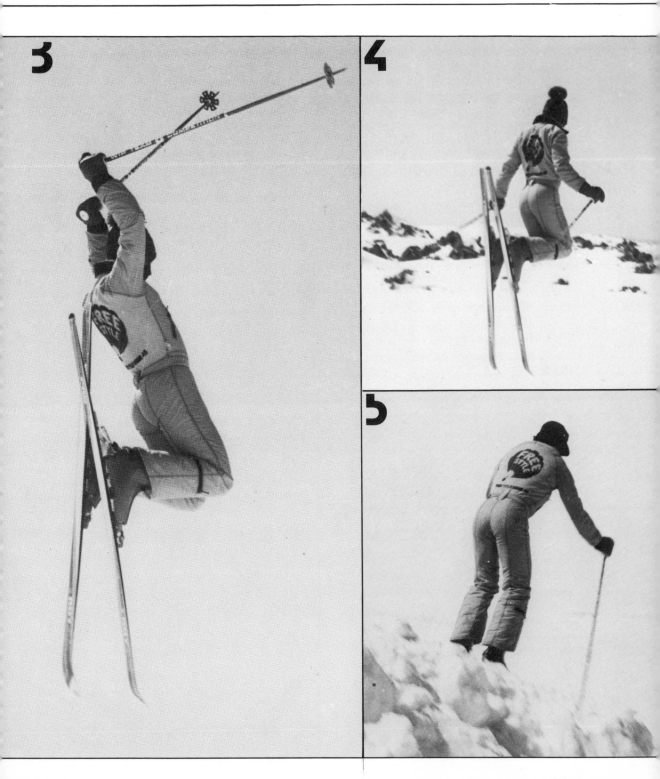

DAFFY

John Clendenin and Johnny Burnett invented this trick in 1965. It is more difficult than a Spread Eagle because it pulls the body slightly to one side and also a tip is placed behind the body, that must be brought forward before landing. Some freestylers looking for something new have landed in Daffy position skiing away on the forward ski, but this is not recommended.

Technique

1 Ski down the inrun, as explained before, with eyes on the lip.

2 Pop off the lip with both legs straight.

3 Once in the air the legs are stretched; one leg behind and one in front. This direction of spreading tends to turn the body sideways in the air and must be compensated for by pulling the arms in the opposite directions. Note how the arm is pulled backwards on the same side as the leg that is stretched forward.

4 The position is held for as long as possible. As the landing approaches the skis come together.

5 A landing is made with the legs absorbing the shock.

Helpful Hints

• All jumps must start with a good pop. Once the pop is completed and the skier is in the air the manoeuvre can be executed.

• The body follows the same trajectory as in all the previous jumps, only a different manoeuvre is performed.

• The Daffy can be best learned on a diving board or trampoline before trying it on snow. If one doesn't have a chance to practise with these facilities learn off the jump by making a small Daffy, and as confidence builds spread the skis further.

• When several Daffys are done in a row it is called a Space Walk.

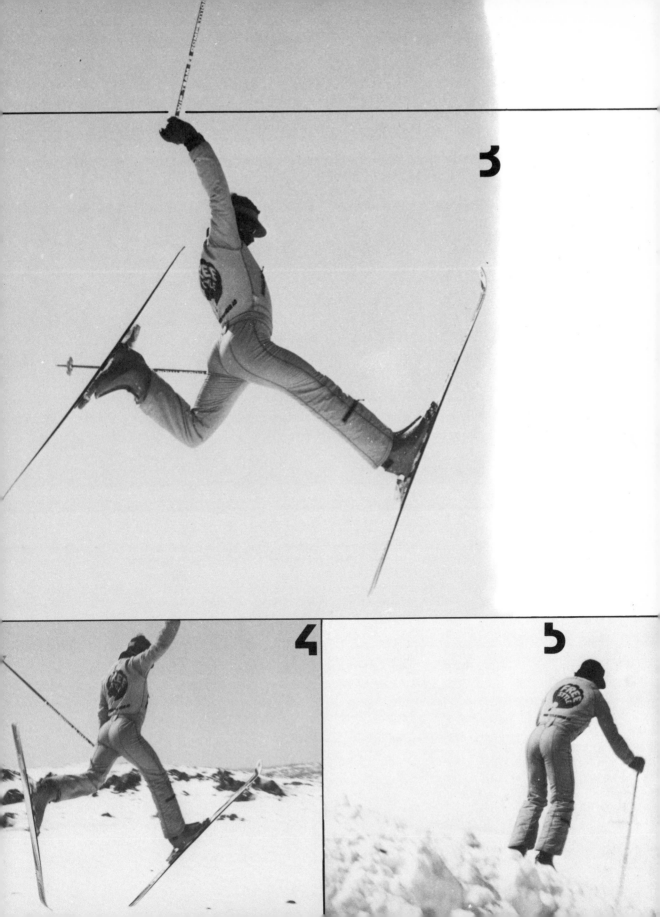

3

5

4

Any single aerial manoeuvre can be repeated as long as one has enough time in the air. A double Daffy makes for an especially flowing double manoeuvre. If one has time four, five or more Daffys can be executed.

2

Technique

1 More speed is needed to ensure enough air time, and a good pop is mandatory. The pop becomes more critical as the distance increases.

2 The skis start to spread.

3 The first Daffy is executed with both arms on the opposite side as the skis.

4 The skis come together.

5 Another Daffy is executed with the arms in the opposite direction as before, keeping the body straight.

Helpful Hints

● Always get off the ramp before starting the trick.

● Once in the air go quickly into the first Daffy so that there is time for the second one.

1

Combinations of different tricks can also be done. In this demonstration a Back Scratcher and a Zudnick have been selected but any two, three, four or more can be used.

Technique

1 A good pop and lots of speed are needed to get the necessary distance to perform double manoeuvres.

2 A Back Scratcher is performed as explained before but this time a bit quicker.

3 The position is quickly released.

4 A Zudnick position.

5 The body straightens in preparation for the landing. The legs absorb the shock.

Helpful Hints

● There is no secret to double manoeuvres. Once the single tricks are mastered, and air sense and confidence increase, double and triple manoeuvres are easily progressed to.

Upright rotational manoeuvres

These days it is not uncommon to be watching a group of skiers coming down the hill when all of a sudden one jumps into the air and rotates a complete 360 degrees, lands on his skis and just keeps skiing. It looks impossible, but for an average to better skier who can do a 360 in tennis shoes and wants to add something really exciting to his skiing ability, a Helicopter or Aerial 360 is within his grasp. Start off by practising aerial 360s without skis or ski boots. If you can jump straight in the air, spin 360 degrees and land straight it is time to try it on skis. If not, try the same exercise by following these steps.

Practise the pop, upward extension, as explained in the upright aerial section—jumping straight into the air keeping the legs extended until coming back to the ground. Use the arms to gain added height as demonstrated in the Upright Aerial with Pop. Try to jump as high as possible, keeping the legs together and the body straight in the air. Using this same pop jump into the air and spin 360 degrees by bringing the outside arm around and next to the body while rotating the head and shoulders. The spin must be initiated the moment the legs have extended and the body is going up. If done too soon the full pop won't be used and if too late the body won't spin the 360 degrees. This timing is the same as on snow. If the movements don't feel right ask someone to see if they can spot what is wrong. While spinning, the body should be as tight as possible with legs together and arms tucked in close to the body. The legs must be straight while in the air and the body should have as straight an axis as possible.

The next step is on the snow. If possible use a pair of very short skis (130s) at the first two or three attempts. Find a good mogul; one that has a definite peak to it with soft snow on the other side. Use the same movements with the skis as without. Here is where previous aerial experience will help because one has already learned how to make a proper pop off a large kicker. The same thing applies to jumping off a bump. The initiation of the pop and spin must be made off the summit

of the mogul. If the same spin and pop, as used without skis, are started off the peak of a mogul the skis will come most of the way around. Once three quarters of the spin is reached, the right technique is being used and it just takes a little more practice. Several points should be remembered when learning a Helicopter off a mogul. Don't ski into the Helicopter fast, it will only scare you. Slow down and jump high to have the necessary air time to spin. Once in the air keep the body wrapped so as not to slow down the rotation. Always start the spin up the hill. Even if only three quarters of the spin is made the skis will slide the other quarter of the way as long as an upright landing has been made.

Once Helicopters feel comfortable across the fall line try them in the fall line or straight down the hill. This step will teach the necessity of jumping slightly forward so that the skis will arrive flat on landing instead of backwards on the tails. This is an important step before going off a professional jump. When jumping across the hill the distance is short and the slope remains the same angle to the skis. It is not so important to pop forward. The moment one jumps in the fall line the angle of the slope must be compensated for. To prepare this transition step, between the hill and the professional jump, build a small jump about 50 cm high with a flat kicker and a gentle landing hill. Get a feel for the jump by going off it slowly, getting good height with a good pop. To execute a Helicopter follow the same procedure as shown off the professional jump.

A Heli, properly executed off a large ramp is a very technical trick. Three different motions must be initiated off the lip of the ramp. First is the upward pop to get good air, second is the right amount of rotation to spin the body exactly 360 degrees from lip to landing, and third is a forward thrust so that the body moves forward through the air so that a flat landing is made. The third motion is not as important as in the moguls, but should be practised off a small jump before a large one.

HELICOPTER

Technique

1 Approaching the kicker the body is slightly counter rotated in preparation for the initiation of the Heli. At the lip of the ramp the three motions are started—the spin, the pop and the thrust forward, which is in the pop.

2 This stance shows one Heli position but both hands could be tucked into the sides, or both above the head, or both out to the side. In this case the outside arm has been lifted to get extra height and then brought over the head to keep everything in a straight axis.

3 The position is maintained as the body rotates. Note how the skis are flat, whereas "before" they were pointed up and "after" pointed down. This is because the pop was initiated forward to compensate for the different angle of the kicker as compared to the angle of the landing hill.

4 The landing hill approaches and the spin is almost complete. To slow down the rotation of the spin the body can open up, as is happening with the arms here. The legs can also be spread apart to slow down the rotation. A landing is made by absorbing the shock with the knees.

Helpful Hints
• Follow the progression to learn a Heli.
• Aerial 360s off moguls are not difficult and can be learned quickly, especially with good instruction and the will power to go for it. Doing a Heli off a big jump requires a lot more timing and precision, but keep practising and it will come together.

720 HELICOPTER

Double (720) and triple (1080) Helicopters have been performed. To this date no one has done four but anything is possible. A 720 requires a strong pop, a forward thrust as before, but twice the amount of rotation. This tends to throw the body sideways. If single Helis are no problem, and you feel ready for a double, it is best to join a freestyle class where all the technique can be explained and the proper conditions are set by someone who knows.

Inverterted aerials

Flipping has a place all to itself in the sport of freestyle skiing. It is dangerous, inspiring, exciting and beautiful. Today, as in 1971 when skiers were first getting together to perform front and back flips, the aerialists are still a tight group. They all know what it takes to extend one's self to go higher, further and attempt new and more difficult manoeuvres. They are elated with someone else's progress, and feel the pain when someone gets hurt. They are also fully aware of the danger involved and condemn anyone or any activity that makes light of the precautions necessary to keep the sport as safe as possible. Unfortunately freestylers had to learn of these dangers by trial and error and several people were hurt along the way. Now, through the knowledge that comes with experience and study, flipping on skis has become possible for anyone who has a desire to try it. Summer camps and winter classes throughout the world have taught many the thrill of being upside down in the air and then landing safely. Even with all that has been learned, and all the safety precautions that are taken, flipping still has its danger. That's what makes it so exciting. There will always be some risk involved, but with an instructor to show the way through a proper progression the risks have been reduced to a minimum.

The first flippers were skiers who wanted to try something new and different. The first recorded flip was done in Norway in 1907. Until the 1970s, individual skiers in different areas flipped without much thought or discussion on technique. They just tried it and, if it worked, kept on going. Several got to the point of perfecting their flips so that they stood up every time. Stein Eriksen, 1954 F.I.S. world champion, invented the curved kicker that enabled him to perform back and front flips with perfection during the late 50s. In the 60s Hermann Goellner became the first aerialist to perform a double flip and a moebius flip (a flip with a full twist). He was later to win a Chevrolet Stingray at one of the first freestyle competitions that took place in Waterville Valley in Vermont. As competition became tougher, and more aerialists were attempting complicated manoeuvres, more training and preparation was needed. Summer camps became popular with aerialists practising different rotations off anything that would get them into the air. They realised that learning a flip on a diving board or trampoline first and then going on to the snow was safer and quicker than just trying it on snow. Many methods have been worked on to help the beginners as well as the more advanced.

This knowledge is available for those who desire the adventure of learning something new and exciting. To learn the technique of an inverted aerial, one must have the coaching of a professional. It is unwise and unsafe to learn a flip by any other means when so much help is available. For this reason only a brief description of several inverted aerials is given so that one can have an idea of what it is about.

In the air there are three basic rotating positions. The tuck is the tightest position giving the quickest rotation. This is the position used when learning a flip for the first time because it gives the most flexibility and control. A pike position gives medium rotation. In other words the body, when in this position, will rotate slower than when in a tuck because more of the body is extended from the centre of gravity. A layout position offers the slowest rotation. This means that if the same amount of backward or forward thrust is given off a jump the body will spin more quickly in a tuck than in a layout. The different position used depends on which jump is to be performed. A layout position is more difficult than a tuck because of the precision of the take off. A tuck position can be slowed down by extending the body into a layout position, or speeded up by tucking harder. A layout cannot be slowed down if thrown too hard because the body can't be extended any further.

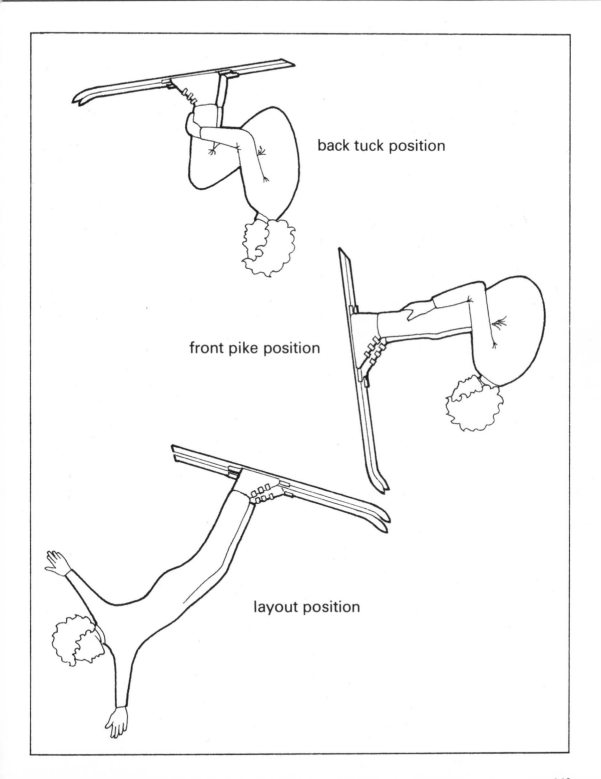

back tuck position

front pike position

layout position

3

Technique

1 Using a front flip kicker the body is launched over the lip. The hands are coming to the knees.

2 In a tuck position the body rotates quickly.

3 As the aerialist feels that he has rotated enough, the body opens to slow down the rotation and prepare for the landing.

4 The landing is made with the knees absorbing the shock.

4

DOUBLE BACK TUCK

Technique

1 The same preparation is made as with a single; the arms are back to prepare for the initiation of the jump.

2 The body extends as though a single is being made, but with more backward rotation.

3 The first flip is made.

4 Halfway through the second, the hands release the tuck and the head is pulled further back to look for the landing.

5 The body extends to slow down the rotation as the landing is spotted.

6 The legs bend to reach the landing.

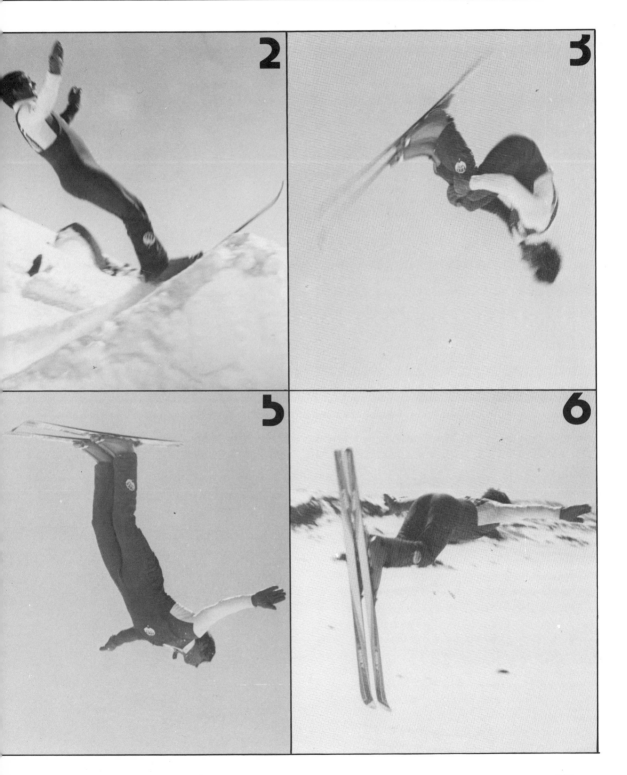

BACK LAYOUT

Technique

1 Down the inrun as with all jumps, relaxed and mind on the lip and manoeuvre, the aerialist heads for the back kicker.

2 The body bends at the knees and the arms come down to prepare for the pop. The pop is being made as the arms and body extend.

3 At the lip the body will be straight with the arms helping the lift. The hips will come forward to give the rotational thrust as the head comes back.

4 The layout position is reached.

5 The legs bend to reach the landing hill.

6 The landing is made.

THE COMPETITIVE EXPERIENCE

As with all sports, top level competition sets the standard for the rest of the sport to follow. Rules and regulations that have governed the international freestyle circuit have provided guide lines for other professional and amateur freestyle competitions throughout the world. The difficult aerial stunts, complicated ballet manoeuvres, and fast mogul skiing have provided a goal for others to strive after. In 1971 the first couple of Hot Dog competitions consisted of one non-stop run where the skier did as much freestyle as possible. It didn't take long for a more comprehensive format to be developed. Freestyle was divided into three disciplines and specific areas were set up for each one. Music became a part of the ballet and mogul events and uniform aerial stages made it safer for jumpers, enabling them to go for more air and more difficult manoeuvres.

The method of judging freestyle competitions has remained much the same since its inception. Between three and five judges grade each competitor. At first a point system from 1 to 20, was used; but as judging became more critical the grading system used for figure skating was adapted. This scoring system extends from 0 to 6 with 6 being the highest, but uses the first decimal. Thus a score could read 3.8 or 5.5. Depending on how many judges there are the high and low scores are either dropped or averaged. The total of the remaining scores is added to find the winner.

To be a winner a freestyler must know what the judges are looking for. For example in the moguls some judges will prefer a more technically smooth run, while others may want to see a more aggressive and attacking style. Though the differences are small they do exist and are found in each of the three disciplines.

Each discipline has its own judging criteria. Three specific characteristics are sought in the bumps: speed, air, turns. Speed used to be judged by how fast the skier appeared to be going but, in the past few years, timing devices have been used so that the speeds of all competitors are precisely known. The judges must then decide on how many jumps were made and how well they were performed. They also score on how well the skier turns the skis to stay in control. These three factors are added up to give an overall score. To win, a competitor must execute good turns at

high speed and still have enough control to jump and perform several aerial manoeuvres. This all takes place down the steepest, bumpiest, most challenging slope available. Course setters try to find a slope that is at least 200 metres long. A narrow path 20 metres wide provides the arena within which the skier must descend. If he skis out of these boundaries he is disqualified. Arriving late or loss of a ski are also grounds for disqualification. After the finish gate a long outrun is left for the skiers to slow down.

Ballet is judged using the same point system as the mogul event but different characteristics are sought. The difficulty of the routine and its smoothness determine a ballet competitor's final score. Difficult tricks, choreographed to music, originality and the overall effect of the routine, are all taken into account. Its smoothness is judged in terms of the lack of falls or signs of imbalance and the harmonious connection of each trick. Each trick should flow into the next without hesitation. When all of this can be put together the result is a great routine. Alan Schoenberger of Utah combined his original Puppet routine with difficult tricks and a flawless execution to win the world ballet title three seasons in a row. With every new season original ideas and more difficult tricks are found in ballet competitions. Many skiers, such as Ernst Garhammer of Germany and Sven Arnbors of Sweden, have contributed a wealth of ideas to the ballet discipline.

This event should take place on an even, gently sloping hill free of obstacles and transitions. A professional ballet arena should be 250 metres long and 50 metres wide, but because this type of slope is hard to find in most areas the longest smoothest slope available is used. The skier is free to use as much of the slope as necessary and in most cases can stop where his routine ends. A music system is set up so that the competitors' chosen music can be played for all to hear. There is no restriction on the length of ski used for ballet in America but in Europe the EFSA (European Freestyle Skiers Association), requires that ballet skis be at least nose high. No other event offers the originality and grace of skis in motion as does the ballet arena.

In contrast to ballet the aerial event offers breathtaking excitement and high flying stunts. Aerial manoeuvres are announced before the competitor takes off so that all know what to expect. Each manoeuvre has been assigned a difficulty co-efficient that compares its level of difficulty to other manoeuvres. For instance, the EFSA gives a single helicopter a difficulty rate of 1.7 while a back flip in layout position is valued at 2.1. These values are arrived at by deciding how much practice is required to perfect the manoeuvre, how dangerous, and how difficult it is. When the aerialist performs his manoeuvre the judge simply has to decide on how well the skier executed that particular jump. Points are given and they are multiplied by the difficulty coefficient to reach a final score. Usually two or three stunts are performed off one, two, or three different aerial stages. The accumulative scores of all jumps are added to decide the winner.

Freestyle is a new sport which began with the first acrobatic competitions in 1971. Its progress in such a short time is incredible. It has adopted principles learned from figure skating, alpine ski racing, ballet, gymnastics, diving and many other sports. As competitions offered more money, more skiers became freestylers. As the level of performance of individual competitors improved so did the need for more organisation and money. Freestyle skiing is now world wide with competitions being held throughout Europe, North America, Australia and New Zealand. Because of these competitions and the professionalism that they create there will be freestylers to keep this new spirit alive for a long time to come.

GLOSSARY

ACTION–COUNTERACTION—(applied to the aerials) the same principle as for every action there is a reaction, except in reverse. When a part of the body is twisted in the air the rest of the body will follow unless force is exerted in the opposite direction.

AERIAL STAGE—the whole jumping arena, including inrun, transition, ramp, landing hill and outrun.

AIR SENSE—the ability to know where the body is positioned in the air in relation to the landing. Air sense is usually acquired with much practice, but some people seem to be born with it.

AIR TIME—the amount of time spent in the air.

ANTICIPATION—(applied to all ski disciplines) to prepare for the beginning of a movement, whether ballet, bumps or aerials. To be thinking ahead of the action.

AXIS—an imaginary straight line on which the body or any object rotates. The closer the parts of the body are to the axis the faster the spin.

BALLET SKI POSITION—an upright stance with arms extended forward as opposed to a normal ski stance where the body is more compact with legs bent.

CHECKING—an edge set to control speed.

COUNTER ROTATION—the twisting of the body in the opposite direction to the actual spin used to initiate the proper rotation.

CROSSOVER POSITION—(applied to ballet) both skis flat on the snow with legs crossed. Also, legs crossed with full weight on one ski as the other is held at an angle over the surface ski.

DOWNHILL SKI—the ski on the downhill side of the slope.

FALL LINE—the line of direct descent down a hill.

HOT DOGGING—what is now freestyle; all three disciplines. Refers also to just the bumps (Hot Dog Run).

INITIATION—start, the beginning of a movement.

INSIDE SKI—(applied to any turn with skis) the ski within the turn.

INVERTED—(applied to aerials) upside down, flipping.

OUTSIDE SKI—(applied to any turn with skis) the ski on the outside of the turn.

SPOTTER—(as in gymnastics) used during flips and somersaults to aid a beginning jumper with the landing. One or two people stand where the jumper will land. If the jumper is going to land too far forward or backward, the spotters assist in cushioning the fall.

SURFACE SKI—the ski that is on the snow as opposed to the one in the air.

TAIL—refers to the back end of the ski.

TIP—refers to the forward end or top of the ski.

UPHILL SKI—the ski that is on the uphill side of the slope.

WIDE STANCE—skis kept more than six inches apart as opposed to a closed stance where boots and legs are pressed together.

WEDGE—(snowplough) a ski stance with the tips together and the tails apart.

INDEX